LEARN TO PLAY GOLF
IN A
Weekend

LEARN TO PLAY GOLF
IN A
Weekend

Edward Craig

hamlyn

For Mum and Eugenie – the toughest twins.

First published in Great Britain in 2005 by
Hamlyn, a division of Octopus Publishing Group Ltd
2–4 Heron Quays, London E14 4JP

'In a Weekend' is the trademark property of Sterling
Publishing Co., Inc., 387 Park Avenue South, New York,
NY 10016, and is used by permission.

ISBN 0 600 61035 7

EAN 9780600610359

A CIP catalogue record for this book is available from the
British Library

Printed in China

10 9 8 7 6 5 4 3 2 1

Photography shot at East Sussex National

contents

Introduction

Nick Faldo took up golf at the age of 14. Watching the all-time greatest golfer Jack Nicklaus winning the 1972 US Masters inspired the youngster to try this sport. Faldo subsequently discovered that he was pretty good at it and six major championship victories later, he is one of the best golfers of all time. Whatever has inspired you to take up this wonderful game, your journey will be an exciting one. You may not end up winning millions on the professional tours or even taking cash regularly from your friends but you are guaranteed hours of fun, frustration and unending challenges.

Learning a new skill is an emotional experience at the best of times. There is the excitement of something new, then the struggle when you realize it might not be as simple as you first thought, followed by the sense of achievement and satisfaction once you are able to hold your own. Any golfer of any age will recognize these feelings.

Taking up golf accentuates these emotions so that your highs are remarkably high, the lows depressingly low and the sense of satisfaction immeasurable. This is why golf has become the pastime of choice for millions of people, and why golf has the broadest arms of any sport. You can play golf in almost any country and men and women compete equally. If you are old enough to walk or young enough to keep walking, you can play and enjoy the game.

The game is simple in concept – hit a ball into a hole in as few shots as possible – but tricky in execution. The best place to start to learn any new skill is with the basics. These are the keys to developing a technique that can allow you the most enjoyment and the least frustration.

This is not as complicated as you might first imagine. The instructions that follow break down the fundamentals into digestible bites. Through use of step-by-step instructions and clear guides, you will learn how to do the simplest things properly – how to stand to the ball, how to grip the club and how to start the swing.

But golf is not only about the swing; there is also instruction on putting, chipping, bunkers, playing from the rough, dealing with the wind and more. The book outlines the basic principles of playing these shots as well as cutting through much of the jargon and conflicting advice you may receive from fellow golfers.

This is not a science, however. There are guidelines that will give you the greatest chance of playing to the limit of your ability but every golf swing is unique and every golfer plays in a different way. This book aims to lay down the basic technical rules in a simple, user-friendly manner.

So whatever your ability, whether you are trying to verse yourself in the fundamentals of the sport or are buying this book as a refresher to sharpen and polish your technique, there will be something of interest and of use. And by the end of the weekend, I hope you will have become as addicted to the magic of the game as the millions of golfers who live, dream and suffer in equal measure every day.

Before you start...

Essential information

This ancient game is not difficult to master, but getting the basics right is the key to success on the fairway. The basic grip and swing are the focus of attention on the first day.

The sport

Welcome to the game of golf. You've made a brave decision. Taking up this most beautiful of sports is far from sensible. Prepare for infuriation, prepare for annoyance, for frustration, for anger but most of all prepare for an unstoppable amount of fun.

Historians dispute the origins of this addictive game – the Dutch and the Scots battle it out – but one thing is certain; someone, more than 500 years ago, had the clever idea of hitting a round, ball-like stone into a hole using a stick. His mate then bet him he could do it in fewer shots. And not much has changed. The sport has spawned a multi-million pound industry, many manicured courses, the science of equipment, the governing bodies, the golf clubs, but golf still comes down to the basic principles, ball-stick-hole.

Golf is not too difficult to master as long as you get the basics right. By getting the simple things right, you can develop a swing and play golf to an enjoyable level relatively quickly. In Day 1 of the book, I will concentrate on the fundamentals, which will stand you in good stead for the rest of your golfing life. There are no good golfers with bad fundamental skills, so conquer these and you are half-way to conquering the sport.

Firstly, and most importantly, we look at your hold on the club. Once you get the grip right, you will avoid many of the problems that plague more experienced golfers. Standing to the ball with athletic posture, playing the ball from the correct position on the ground and making these basics second nature will give you a great launch pad into the game.

Secondly, we will look at the basic swing: the first movements, the backswing and through-swing. It is always dangerous to over-analyze what should be a free-flowing, reactive and natural motion, which is why the fundamentals are so important. By the end of the first day, you will have a basic understanding of how to strike a golf ball and that is the very essence of the game.

Good clubs are not too costly, will last a long time and provide the building blocks of a good game.

The course

A typical golf course is made up of a number of elements. First, there is the clubhouse where you can change, prepare for the game, usually get a bite to eat and indulge in post-match analysis. You will find a pro-shop with a resident teaching professional who will be able to offer you advice on your game and on the course, give lessons, sell equipment and generally be the recognized expert.

Courses will either be 18 or 9 holes long. Each hole has a 'par'. This is the number of shots that a professional golfer should take on that particular hole – all holes are either par-3s, par-4s or par-5s. A course will then have an overall 'par', the number of shots a professional expects to take in total; typically, this is around 72.

Each hole has a number of elements to it. You start on a 'tee-box', a flat area with markers from where you hit your first shot. Most holes have a 'fairway', an area of closely mown grass from where you will want to hit your second shot, unless you are playing a short par-3 hole and have managed to hit the green with your tee shot. If you have missed the fairway you might be in the 'rough', the longer grass placed there to trap your ball, making it hard to make a clean strike. Rough varies in length, usually getting thicker the further you are from the fairway. You then reach the 'green', the manicured and smooth area of very short grass with a hole cut onto it. You should only use your putter on the green to avoid taking divots (holes in the grass). The green and fairway may have 'bunkers' on them; sizeable holes filled with sand, designed as traps to gather your ball and make life awkward. There may well be water in the form of streams, ponds or lakes and there are all sorts of penalties if you are unfortunate enough to send your ball swimming.

This is the basic make-up of the course and club but there are numerous rules and ways of behaving that make a round of golf safe, enjoyable, fair and competitive. The principle, though, has not changed. You want to get the ball into the hole in as few shots as possible!

Which course to take?

There are numerous different types of courses with their own distinctive challenges and variations. The classic course is a links, carved out of the sand-dunes that join the shore with the sea. Golf is said to have begun on this terrain. Other types of courses are parkland courses which are inland and tree-lined; heathland courses surrounded by heather; and resort courses which are found throughout the US and increasingly in Europe. These are manufactured layouts with big shallow bunkers, lots of water and wide fairways. Most golfers prefer one type to another. It is this richness and variety that makes the sport so well-loved globally.

The rules

Golf is a game of rules. The *Rules Book* itself is a relatively digestible tome, but the vagaries that the sport throws up have compelled the R&A (the golf world's governing body, based at the Royal and Ancient at St Andrew's, Scotland) to publish *Decisions on the Rules of Golf* – a lengthy publication that outlines the decisions the R&A has made on complicated situations.

Buy a *Rules Book* and have a flick through. There are 34 rules broken into various sub-sections, appendices and notes. They cover everything from equipment to penalties in hazards. Make sure you have some understanding of the regulations before playing a round so you not only know when you have infringed the rules, but also what you can get away with and how the rules can be used to your advantage.

There are three basic principles that you should bear in mind:

- Play the ball as it lies
- Play the course as you find it
- And finally, if in doubt, do what is fair.

The rules are what makes golf such a respected game. Cheating is considered an unforgivable sin as golf is a self-regulating sport; the participants must own up to all infringements and call penalties on themselves. Failing to do so can lead you into serious disgrace with other golfers.

Make sure you have a basic understanding of the rules as laid down by the R&A and the USGA, golf's governing bodies which operate on behalf of millions of golfers across the world.

Etiquette

Golf is such a pleasant experience, free of the outward aggression prevalent in other sports because there is a strict code of conduct – etiquette. It is etiquette that makes players call penalties on themselves; etiquette keeps the game safe and ensures that you behave reasonably towards your opponent. Here are the basic rules of etiquette that you need to adhere to on the course:

- Never make noise while another golfer is playing. Keep perfectly still and do not stand directly behind them, whether you are on the green, fairway or tee.
- Play quickly – do not hold up the group behind and keep in touch with the group in front. Take as long as you need over a shot, but walk briskly between shots – slow play is the most irritating thing about golf. Let groups behind you play through if you are holding them up.

Etiquette requires that you repair any divots and pitch-marks you've caused before you move on.

- Repair divots, pitch-marks (marks made by your ball landing on the green) and rake bunkers once you've been in them.
- Never leave your bag on a green or tee-box. When on the green it is best to leave bags near the next tee to save time.

You'll pick up the rest quite quickly once you start playing but as advance warning, read the 10 main rules outlined on pages 12–13. These will keep you on the straight and narrow when you step on a course for the first time.

Many courses have a dress-code so be wary of this when turning up to a new place in jeans and trainers. It is best to dress smartly when playing, as it is a disciplined game. Dressing more formally will put you in the frame of mind needed to play well.

Finally, always play safely. Wait until the group in front of you is out of range before hitting, even if you are being pressed by the group behind. Before you take a swing, make sure there is no one in range whom you might strike with either ball or club. If your ball is heading for a group nearby, yell 'Fore!' at the top of your voice – this should give them a chance to take cover.

The rules and etiquette may appear to take some of the fun out of the sport by imposing archaic discipline but the more you play the more you will appreciate their importance.

Stand still and quiet while your partner is taking a shot or you will disturb them. Do not stand directly behind the person taking the shot.

The 10 most crucial rules

The penalties

Penalties for infringement of the rules can vary depending on the type of match you are playing. If you are playing matchplay (see jargon busting opposite) the penalty will differ from that used if you are playing strokeplay. So before you mark your card in error or offer your opponent the hole, check to see you have applied the right penalty.

On the tee

1 Your bag

You are only allowed to carry 14 clubs in your bag during a competition or match. If you discover you have left in an old putter by accident and are carrying 15 clubs, then in matchplay you lose each hole played with the erroneous club in your bag. In strokeplay, you have to add two penalty strokes for each hole played with an extra club, as famously happened to the luckless Ian Woosnam during the 2001 Open Championship at Royal Lytham and St Anne's, just as he had moved into the lead. The two-stroke penalty (he discovered it on the second hole) cost him the tournament.

2 The honour

This is who has the right to play first from the tee. It is usually the player who had the best score on the previous hole. If you play out of turn in matchplay, your opponent can ask you to replay the shot at no penalty. On the fairway and on the greens the golfer to play is the one furthest from the hole.

3 Taking provisions

If you play a wild shot from the tee or anywhere else on the course, and are unsure whether you'll find the ball, you are allowed to play a provisional ball. You play the shot from the same place and then have five minutes to find your original ball from when you start looking. If you cannot find your original ball, declare it lost at a penalty of two shots and play your provisional – which means that you will be playing your fourth shot.

4 Out of bounds

If you hit your tee-shot or any other shot over the boundary of the course, from where you are forbidden to play, then you must replay the shot from the original position at a penalty of one stroke.

5 Hazards

The main rule when you are playing from a hazard, whether a bunker or stream, is that you are not allowed to ground your club before playing the shot. Even if you rest on your club as you are waiting for your turn to play, you are breaching this rule and the penalty is one shot in both matchplay and strokeplay. The club cannot touch the sand in a bunker during either your backswing or practice swing.

If in doubt about whether you can move the ball or not, play it as it lies.

6 The unplayable ball

If you decide that your ball is in a position from which it is impossible to play and you cannot dream of making contact or getting a proper swing at it, you will have to deem it unplayable. You now have three options for a penalty drop:
● Drop the ball two club-lengths away and no nearer the hole
● Play from where you originally hit the ball before landing yourself in trouble
● Draw an imaginary line from the hole to your ball and extend it back beyond your ball – you can drop as far back as you like.

The penalty for a drop is one stroke.

7 Immovable obstruction

You can land behind trees, in bunkers or dunk your ball into the water and you have to bite the bullet and play on. But if your ball finishes near an artificial hazard such as a sprinkler-head or a post in the ground, you can take a free drop if the object is impeding your swing or stance.

8 Water hazards

If your ball goes for a swim, you have three options:

● Play it – this is only possible in shallow water and is inadvisable
● Replay the shot from where you hit into the water
● Drop the ball two club-lengths back on a line from where it entered the water. Lateral water hazards, marked by red-stakes and usually along the side of a hole, allow you to drop on the other side of the water as long as you are no nearer the hole. You can never drop nearer the hole in any situation. When you land in the water you incur a penalty of one stroke in both matchplay and strokeplay.

On the green

9 Marking on the green

You can mark your ball, pick it up and clean it once you are on the putting surface. If your marker is on the line of someone else's putt, you are allowed to move it using your putterhead as a measure, but make sure you putt from the original spot or you will be penalized. You can remove sand, repair pitchmarks, move twigs and leaves from the line of your putt, but you musn't tap in spike marks.

10 Flagstick trouble

Once your ball is on the putting surface, it must not touch the flagstick on its way to the hole. This means that, so long as you can see the hole, you should remove the flag before playing. If you are faced with a long putt then you can ask your playing partner or caddie to attend the flag. They must remove it from the hole before the ball drops; otherwise you will incur a two-stroke penalty.

Your ball cannot strike the flagstick if you are putting from the green.

Other rules

Local rules On any particular course, there will be a number of places where boundaries, hazards or certain situations are indistinct. If a hole runs alongside a beach, is this out of bounds, for instance? On the back of a scorecard a club will publish Local Rules, which explain rulings for common situations. It is important to pay attention to these before you play so you have a full picture of the challenges ahead. More often than not, you can make them work to your advantage.

Winter rules A club may decide to play winter rules. This is a preservation measure, as well as making the game fairer when the condition of the course is poor, that allows the player to improve the lie of the ball on the fairway. Usually, you can lift, clean and place the ball before playing your shot, although you must not place the ball any nearer the hole.

Equipment

What's in a golf bag?

Golf clubs are not as expensive as you might think and a set of clubs will last a long time, so any initial outlay is an investment in your golfing future.

The driver

This is the most exciting club in the bag – the long-stick, used for hitting the ball as far as you can. Nowadays, drivers are often made from a lightweight metal called titanium and have enormous heads. Drivers have a loft (see jargon busting) of between seven and eleven degrees. The more lofted the driver, the further the ball flies.

A typical bag

Club	Description
Driver	Longest club in the bag, biggest head
3-wood	Big, bulky head, shorter shaft than a driver
5-wood	A smaller head than 3-wood and shorter shaft
Irons 3–9	Thin metal heads with changing lofts – the higher the number of the iron, the more loft
Pitching-wedge	Rounded and lofted iron
Sand-wedge	Rounded iron with a flat bottom and lots of loft
Lob-wedge	Similar to sand-wedge but with yet more loft
Putter	Usually a shorter club with a square grip and a head that has no loft

> ### Jargon busting
>
> **Loft** The angle the club sits at relative to the perpendicular and which determines the ball's flight.
> **Club-head** The part of the club used to strike the ball.
> **Shaft** The part of the club that runs from grip to club-head.

The driver, used to hit long distances, and the woods, of various weights and sizes, are the most exciting clubs in the bag.

Different types of irons

There are primarily two types of iron clubs – blades and cavity-backs. Blades are the old-fashioned, clean-looking clubs with an almost straight back. Cavities have a hollow back – hence the name. Blades were the original club and feel fantastic if you catch the ball cleanly with them – but they are difficult to hit well and cause painful vibrations if you catch them wrong. Cavity-back clubs are best suited to beginners and handicap golfers as they offer much more forgiveness for off-centre strikes. Most clubs sold nowadays are cavity-backed.

Cavity-backed blades (left) are more forgiving of off-centre strikes than bladed irons (right).

3-wood and 5-wood

These fairway woods are designed to be hit from short grass. They are easy to play with and will typically be used on par-5s or long par-4s for approach shots over 182m (200yd). A 3-wood is also great to use from the tee as it is easier to hit the ball straight.

3–4 irons

These long irons are, typically, used for 164–182m (180–200yd) shots. They are notoriously difficult to play well, although there is no better feeling in golf than really catching a 3-iron.

5–7 irons

Mid-irons should be used for 136–164m (150–180 yd) shots to the green. If you are confident with your mid-irons you can rescue wayward and short drives easily, as well as attacking par-3s aggressively.

8–9 irons

Short-irons should be used for 88–127m (130–140 yd) shots to the green. You should be fond of your short-irons as they set up a lot of scoring opportunities.

Rescue clubs

The rescue club is a relatively new animal by which many golfers now swear. It is a hybrid iron/wood that is used for hitting longer 164–182m (180–200yd) shots. A rescue club gets its name from how simple it is to strike from bad lies – when you are in the rough or on a bare patch of fairway. Where you may have wanted to chip out sideways before, a rescue club gives you the option of moving the ball significantly forward.

Wedges

Wedges, like drivers, are specialist clubs that give you great control and feel around the greens as well as from 110m (120yd) and closer. Manufacturers have ploughed money into perfecting wedges and there are as many available as there are drivers or putters. They are usually beautifully crafted clubs, with a shiny finish. Tour golfers have taken to playing with as many as four wedges in their bags to add versatility close to the greens.

Pitching-wedges

The pitching-wedge will have 48° loft and will come as part of your set of irons. Once your game is up to a certain level, it is worth investing in a specialist pitching-wedge. You will use this club for chipping and pitching out of trouble, as well as full approach shots from around 91m (100yd) out.

Use your sand-wedge for escaping from greenside bunkers, but it is also useful for chipping and pitching.

Sand- and lob-wedges

These are very specialized clubs that should be bought separately from your set. Use a sand-wedge predominantly for escaping from greenside bunkers. Its rounded sole makes it adept at skipping through the sand. But it is also a versatile club when used for chipping and pitching around the green as long as the lie is not too bare.

A lob-wedge is also a useful tool for the sand. Many players will turn to this club ahead of the sand-wedge, as it adds an extra dimension to the shots you can play around the green. It is probably best to pick up a lob-wedge after you've developed a solid short game – in the wrong hands it is dangerous!

A pitching-wedge will typically have 48° loft and will help you chip and pitch out of trouble.

A lob-wedge is useful in the sand if used in the right hands. Wait until you have developed your game before acquiring one.

A good grip (bottom) is crucial to playing well; worn grips (top) can alter your control and may impede your swing.

Shafts

The shaft is the most important element of the club – it is the engine that drives the club. It is crucial to find a shaft that suits your swing, which means using shafts of the right flex. A flexible shaft is more suited to beginners and lady golfers who cannot swing the club as fast as more experienced players. Tour players will use a variety of stiff shafts, but they have highly tuned techniques that make the most of this technology. Most handicap golfers would do best using more flexible shafts.

Grips

Your only contact with the club is your grip, which is why you will play less well the more worn it gets. It is difficult to keep control of the club-head if the grip is moving around in your hands. If you have to hold on tightly to stop the club flying down the fairway after the ball, you will impede your swing. Most golf shops will offer a regripping service that can instantly improve your game.

No one putter will suit all golfers. Buy one that feels comfortable.

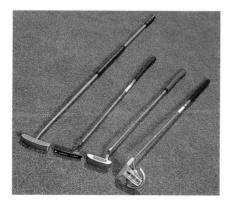

There are thousands of putter designs. Try various types to find one that suits you.

Putters

There are so many different types of putters that we can only scratch the surface on the designs and various merits of this most mysterious of clubs. Here are three rules for selecting a putter:

- Make sure the shaft is the right length
- Don't buy the most expensive or famous putter, just because it is expensive and famous
- Comfort is the most important thing, whatever the club's looks or cost.

The basic principle when it comes to putting is that we are all different. No one putter suits everyone, despite marketing talk and advertisements.

Belly-putters and Broom-handles

Recently, these putters have established themselves as viable options in the putter market, where before there was an embarrassed stigma attached to them. The broom-handle putter is an extra-long club that either rests under your chin or in your chest. It splits your hands up and takes your wrists out of the stroke. A belly-putter rests in your stomach and you hold it like a normal putter. This extra anchor provides a stable base for putting.

Experiment with different makes of ball to find out which suits you best. Each type has varying properties and the right ball can help your game, but only once your swing is proficient.

Get the ball rolling

Equipment manufacturers will make you believe you can buy a better game. To a certain extent, this is true – decent woods and irons can make golf more forgiving and fun but you do need to have half-decent technique before you can make the most of the new technology. Nowhere is this more obvious than with the ball-manufacturing industry. Advances in ball design and technology have changed the face of golf at the highest level over the last five years. Balls now fly further and straighter than they ever did before.

Once you can swing a club proficiently, it is crucial to find a type of ball that you like and with which you are comfortable. Most ball manufacturers will promise high-spinning, extra distance, soft-feel balls on the packaging. The only way to find out if you agree is to try them.

Balls do perform differently, so use one variety of ball under various conditions until you learn its idiosyncrasies. Some are softer than others and give you more feel but will not fly as far (three-piece balls). The harder (and cheaper) balls will bounce miles down the fairway (two-piece), but may do the same through the green. The key is to practise with one type of ball and you will become used to its consistency and effects quickly.

Accessories

Golf is a sport of accessories. You can fill your bag up with an enormous amount of useful and useless gadgets and gizmos to help you on your way round. There are, however, some essential accessories that you can't do without:

Tees

You use tees to tee the ball up on the teeing ground at the start of each hole. Tees are the accessory that makes hitting golf balls easiest. They come in different lengths and may be wooden or plastic. There are a number of tee-makers who have tried to revolutionize this simple aid with various additions and modifications, but none have caught on. As a result, this is one area of the game that is untouched by technology – at the moment.

Ball markers

Plastic or metal circles, often designed with club logos, used for marking the ball on the green. A small coin can also be used to mark your ball.

Pitch-mark repairers

A tool used to repair the mark your ball makes once it lands on the green. Never repair one mark, always repair two – this will help maintain the standard of the greens and keep you friendly with the greenkeeper.

Gloves

Have at least two gloves in your bag in case one gets wet or damaged. You wear a glove on your left (or top) hand to give you added grip and protection against blisters during a round.

Other toys and gizmos

You could write a short book on the other tools that manufacturers have come up with to fill golf bags. From blinkers for sunglasses to instant green readers, automatic ball cleaners to on-bag drinks dispensers – you name it and it has probably been invented. While these make great stocking fillers for golf enthusiasts, they are non-essential bits of kit and, in all honesty, are more fun than useful.

Some accessories, such as gloves, tees, ball markers and pitch-mark repairers, are vital additions to the golf bag and cannot be done without. However, there are hosts of gadgets and gizmos that are fun rather than necessary.

Different forms of golf

Golf is played in a number of different formats. Every golfer has a preference for a particular version of the game; listed below are some of the most common forms:

Strokeplay

Most professional tournaments, except the Ryder Cup and the occasional matchplay event, take this format. Quite simply, the person who takes the fewest number of shots wins. This may be over four days and four rounds, like the Majors (see page 21), or through 18 holes. Handicaps may apply in strokeplay, so the player with the lowest net-score (the score once their handicap is deducted) wins; handicaps are never used in professional events.

Matchplay

Matchplay is when players go head-to-head, competing for individual holes, instead of overall lowest score. Usually, players play as singles, comparing scores at the end of the hole, not the end of the round. If you win the first hole, you are 1-up. If you win the second, you are 2-up. But as soon as your opponent starts winning holes back, this score gets shaved and you go back to 1-up, then all square (level terms) and so on. You keep going until one player is more holes up than there remain holes to play – so if you are 3-up on the seventeenth tee, you have won 3 and 2 (three ahead with only two holes left).

Stableford

This is a system of scoring that is often used in corporate events. It is essentially strokeplay, but instead of marking the number of strokes you played on any particular hole, you score points.

The points system is worked out by your net-score (after the handicap is deducted) relative to the par of any particular hole. You will receive two points for a net-par, one point for a net-bogey and no points for anything worse. Birdies earn you three points, eagles four and so on. For example, if you are playing a par-4 where you receive two strokes, if you make a six, you deduct your two shots, so your net score is four – this is a net-par and in Stableford you would score two points. If you made a five, your net score is three – a net birdie, so you will receive three points – and so on. A birdie is a score of one under the par of the hole and an eagle is a score of two under the par. If you are ever lucky enough to make an albatross you have holed your second shot on a par-5 – this is more rare than a hole-in-one.

This is a popular system as it allows for that nightmare hole where you take 10 – you just get no points rather than ruining a pure strokeplay card.

Your choice of game format will affect how scores are calculated. Every golfer has his or her own favourite version.

Fourball

When four golfers play their own ball in the round, they are playing a fourball. This is usually played in pairs where the lowest score between you and your partner counts for that hole. This can be played in a matchplay or strokeplay format. In the US, fourballs are also know as foursomes, which can be confusing, because in Europe a foursome is something different (see below).

Foursomes

Again, there are four golfers playing in pairs but instead of hitting their own balls, they take it in turns to play one ball for each pair. At the beginning of the round, one player from each side elects to play the odd-numbered holes and one the even-numbers. From then on, the players take alternate strokes. Again, as with fourball, this can take the format of a strokeplay or matchplay event. This is a challenging format as you have to deal with the vagaries of someone else's game as well as your own.

Greensomes

A similar format to foursomes, but instead of taking alternate shots from the tee, everyone drives, each pair selects the best drive, the other is picked up, and you play alternate shots from there until you hole out. Again, this may be used in a strokeplay or matchplay format.

The Majors and Ryder Cup

There are four major golf tournaments played each year: the Masters, the US Open, the Open Championship and the PGA Championship. All except the Open Championship (know as the British Open in the US) are played in the USA. They are all strokeplay events and professional golfers measure their career success by their performances in the majors. Many good golfers have not won a big one, which can become a real burden.

The Ryder Cup happens every two years and is a team event played between the US and Europe. It is played over three days, with points awarded to the winning players of a variety of singles matches, foursomes and fourballs. All these games are matchplay in each game, and the team that wins the most number of holes wins the match – as opposed to strokeplay, where the golfer who plays the least shots to complete a set number of holes, wins. To qualify for the Ryder Cup is a huge achievement and the pinnacle of many professional golfers' careers. The cup is named after Samuel Ryder, who paid the expenses for a professional match between the United States of America and Great Britain in 1927. He wished it to be played 'in the name of friendship and honest competition'.

Scramble

This is a version of the game popular in the US. You play in teams of four, everyone drives and you select the best drive, picking up the others. Then everyone plays one shot from where the best drive finished. Again, you select the best shot out of these four and continue until you hole out. This should be a low-scoring version of the game as you have four tries for any one shot.

Questions people ask

A few lessons with a professional will help establish solid fundamentals and allow you to enjoy the game more quickly.

Is golf an expensive sport?

No, not if you don't want it to be. The initial outlay for buying clubs can be steep, but you could and should, if you are a beginner, buy a second-hand half-set of clubs, which will not cost too much. These are available from most golf shops. The extra expense is on buying clothes, shoes, balls and green fees. Once you have your golfing clothes and shoes, these will last a long time. Balls can be expensive, especially as you may lose a few when you first start, but there are budget balls available which are perfect for beginners. The cost of green fees depends on the course you are playing but you will always find cheaper courses.

Do you have to be a member of a club to play golf?

No. There is a common misconception that this is the case. Being a member of a club can be fun socially and will allow you to play in club competitions as well as get a handicap. All these things are possible without joining a club, which can be an expensive and difficult option. Increasingly, there is a nomadic population of golfers who pay as they play without being members – a cheaper and more versatile option.

Do I need a handicap to play golf?

No, but once you reach a certain standard, it is advisable to get a handicap. This is most easily done if you are a member of a club, but many national governing bodies will run non-membership handicap schemes. The advantage of having a handicap is that it will allow you to play in amateur competitions, and gives an indication of your ability so you are able to compete against opponents of a different standard. Occasionally, if you are a visitor at a club, they will ask to see your handicap certificate to check you know your way around a golf course, but this is increasingly rare.

Do I need lessons?

Every beginner needs to build their golf swing on solid fundamentals and although this publication will guide you in the right direction, it is no substitute for lessons. In many countries, beginner sessions can be taken free of charge, either in a group or individually and this is an essential way to start a fruitful and enjoyable golfing life.

Is golf an old man's sport?

No. Golf can be played by anyone from the age of eight to eighty and beyond. It is one of the best sports that men and women can play together and it has an increasingly youthful playing base. The leisurely pace of the game is an ideal distraction for young and old alike, and characters like Tiger Woods and Annika Sorenstam are opening up the sport to a previously untapped market.

Golf can be played by anyone of any age from eight to eighty and the game has attracted many new players.

Is the game very elitist?

Not on the whole, but it does have its elitist elements. Regrettably, there are still men-only clubs, but these are slowly becoming extinct like the dinosaurs that govern such institutions. There are exclusive clubs where it either costs a fortune to join or you have to know the right person, go to the right school etc. Luckily, golf as an industry has realized that this helps no one and it is becoming much easier to be a member of a club, to find a decent course on which to play and to enjoy the greatest sport on the planet.

Is there a dress-code?

Many golf courses do have dress-codes, which is no bad thing as it reflects the discipline and control required to play good golf. Many public courses may have a relaxed attitude to golf, but dressing smartly and looking the part is one of the pleasures of the game. You wouldn't play soccer in jeans – so, likewise, golf has its own, inventive, varied and fun, dress-code.

Is it a difficult game to learn?

Golf is best described as an easy game to play badly! This means that you can pick up the sport with a bit of diligence and practice relatively quickly, so that you can hold your own on the course and enjoy the various thrills and spills the game throws at you. But to become an expert, low-handicap golfer does require skill, time and practice. We can all have a lot of fun, but winning the Masters doesn't happen to everyone.

Golf is one of the best sports that men and women can play together on an equal footing since it is a game of skill rather than brute force.

Day 1: The basic swing

DAY 1

The basic swing

The aims of Day 1 are to learn how to:

- Hold the club correctly
- Set up to the ball correctly
- Build a solid backswing
- Develop a good downswing and finish.

The golf swing may look like a complicated motion of twisting arms, turning backs and an explosive release of power. In fact, it is a very natural movement – the modern swing is a simple, instinctive motion, relying on easy movements that everyone can do.

The root of a successful swing is solid basics. The first two lessons concentrate on grip and set-up and once you have mastered these fundamentals, practising until they have become natural and comfortable, you are on your way to an easier golfing life.

Lessons 3 and 4 look at the golf swing itself, running through the basic ideas and techniques behind a solid and consistent movement, as well as highlighting common dangers and difficulties faced by golfers.

By the end of Day 1, you will have developed an understanding of the techniques used in the golf swing and what it feels like to strike a ball sweetly. Once you've struck your first shot off the middle of the club, you will be hooked.

How difficult can it really be?

Welsh golfing legend Ian Woosnam, who won the US Masters in 1991, described the swing as two turns and a swish. All he meant by this was that during the swing you turn your body back and then turn it through, with the arms and hands releasing at impact, swishing the ball straight down the middle. His point was that many golfers over-complicate what is a simple, natural motion.

Over-analyzing positions in the swing and the minute detail of small movements can lead to an age-old problem: paralysis by analysis. Golfers become so preoccupied by technique that they cannot move for fear of getting it wrong – they forget the natural instincts that produce flair, invention and rhythm.

So take a step back and consider what you are doing – trying to whack a ball into a hole in as few shots as possible.

The grip

🕐 **10 minutes**

🚩 **Goal** To learn a correct grip, the difference between types of grips and to develop a comfortable grip

Difficulty rating ⚪⚪⚪⚪⚪

The importance of a good grip cannot be stressed strongly enough – this is the first and most simple technique that you need to master. Get it right and many of golf's problems will never trouble you. It is your one connection with the club, your only link to how the ball will fly; a good grip lets your hands work together – as one – in the swing, not against each other.

Don't choke the bird

Many golfers will hold the club too tightly, causing tension in their arms, which restricts movement in the rest of the swing. Hold the club gently, as though you are holding a small bird. You don't want to crush the bird but you don't want to let it escape either. Likewise with the golf club, don't crush the grip but don't let it escape.

Correct grip

1
First, position your left hand on the club. The grip should run from the base of your middle finger to the middle of your index finger. Do not let the club slip into the palm of your hand.

2
Now, close your fingers round the club. When you look down at your hand you should only be able to see two knuckles, with the logo on your glove facing the target.

Vardon   Interlocking   Baseball

3

Bring your right hand on to the club. The grip should run through the bottom half of your fingers and not be in the palm. The left-hand thumb sits in the pad of your right-hand thumb.

4

The 'V' of your right hand should point to your right shoulder with your right thumb pointing to the left of the centre of the shaft. How you interlock your little finger on the right hand decides what grip you will use.

Three choices

There are three recognized and orthodox methods of holding the golf club. The most common technique is the Vardon (or overlapping) grip, favoured by the majority of golfers. There are also the interlocking and baseball grips – choose your grip for one reason: comfort. Practise with all three and you'll soon realize which one is the right one for you.

Vardon grip The little finger of the right hand overlaps the index finger of the left.
Interlocking grip The little finger of the right hand interlocks with the index finger of the left, a method used by Tiger Woods and Jack Nicklaus. Golfers with smaller hands find this more comfortable.
Baseball grip The little finger and index fingers do not interlock at all; a rare choice and more suitable for junior golfers who are learning the game.

Common problems

The ideal grip is 'neutral', which means that the left and right hands work together with neither having more influence on the club than the other. A neutral grip makes the club-face aim straight down the ball-to-target line when you set up, which is known as being square. As you swing, the club-face will remain square, so that at impact it is aiming straight at the target and producing straight shots. If you have a weak or strong grip, it is more difficult to have the club-head square at impact, making it hard to hit consistent shots.

Jargon busting

A neutral grip Allows the hands to work in unison in the swing with neither having more influence than the other.
A strong grip Makes the hands too prominent in the swing.
A weak grip Makes it hard to use the hands through the swing.
Ball-to-target line or target line An imaginary line from where you want to hit to where you want the ball to go.

Grips to avoid

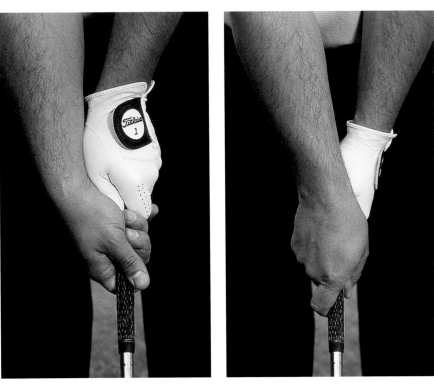

The strong grip
With a strong grip, when you look down, you can see four knuckles on the back of the left hand. Consequently, the right hand turns underneath the club as though it is pulling the accelerator of a motorbike. A strong grip is likely to make you hit a hook – a shot curving viciously left once hit.

The weak grip
With a weak grip you cannot see any knuckles on the back of the left hand and the right hand comes over the top of the grip too much, with its back almost facing the sky. This could easily lead to sliced shots – the ball curves right, usually into some thick rough.

Understanding the neutral grip

Try this practice to understand the importance of a neutral grip.

Stand as though you are addressing the ball before swinging, place your hands together without a golf club, so that they face each other, with the back of your left hand pointing at what would be the target. Swing your arms as though you are swinging a club. At the point of 'impact', your hands will naturally point downwards, with the back of your left hand facing the target again. If you were holding a club, you would have started with the face square to the target and a neutral grip. So at impact the club-face stays square when your hands reach their natural impact position.

If you started with a strong grip, your hands would still return to that neutral and natural position at impact. But the club-face would be closed – or aiming left – because it was only square with the strong grip you had at address. If you started with a weak grip, your club-face would be open and the ball could disappear right.

Practice tip
Practising your grip is the simplest practice time you will ever spend. Leave a club in the hall at home and each time you pass it, spend 30 seconds refining your grip and making it feel more natural. The more you hold a club with a good grip, the more that grip will become second nature to you.

Practice drill Achieving a neutral grip

1
Take an address position, and without a club, place your hands together pointing at what would be the target.

2
Swing your arms as though swinging a club. Note at impact that your hands will naturally point downwards.

The set-up

🕐 **1 hour**

⚑ **Goal** To develop strong posture, good alignment and understand ball position

Difficulty rating ⬤⬤⬤○○
It takes time and practice to develop a comfortable and consistent set-up position

Good fundamentals come down to four things: grip, posture, alignment and ball position. Now you can hold the club correctly and confidently, you must learn how to set up for a shot accurately.

The key to consistency comes from decent posture. If you have a strong and athletic address position, you will swing more accurately, using only the muscles required to hit a ball well. Weak positioning can lead to either a busy swing, with flailing arms and overactive legs causing random striking or a completely rigid movement, making it hard to generate sufficient power.

Practice drill Achieving a good set-up

1
Stand up straight, take hold of the club, make a good grip and hold it out horizontally in front of you. Keep your feet a shoulder-width apart and have your toes turned out slightly.

2
Now bend from your hips and your hips alone, keeping your back straight and letting the club drop to the ground so its sole is flat on the ground. You want your arms to hang naturally under your shoulders.

> **Jargon busting**
>
> **Posture** How you stand to the ball and the shape your body takes at address.
> **Alignment** Where your body aims in the swing.
> **Stance** How wide apart your feet are positioned and the ball's position in relation to your body at address.

Common errors Set-up

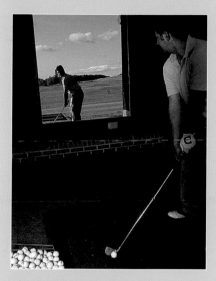

3
From this position, flex your knees so that your bottom sticks out slightly. You should have a hand's width between your grip and your thighs. Keep your chin up from your chest and get comfortable.

Posture too upright
Don't be too upright in your posture. It is important to have a nice straight back and to develop clear angles between your lower and upper body but don't let your knees straighten – retain the flex, otherwise you will create a stiff swing.

Over flexing
Don't flex too much and stoop over the ball, as you will find a weak position causes unnecessary motion. You want enough knee flex to allow controlled movement in the swing.

Posture check

Use a mirror to check your posture. Take your address position as though you are hitting at the mirror. Keep an eye on your angles – is your bottom sticking out, is your back straight, do you have enough knee flex? Turn round and check as though you are hitting away from the mirror.

Throughout your golfing life, keep an eye on your posture using a mirror, reflections or a friend who understands good posture. The more golf you play, the easier it is to slip into bad habits, causing problems to your game.

Aiming accurately

The next part of your set-up that you need to master is alignment. Without good alignment, it is impossible to be accurate. If you are misaligned, you may try to compensate for what will be an inaccurate shot by altering your swing, which could well lead to a wild hit.

Of all the fundamental techniques relating to the golf swing, accurate alignment is the one that requires the most work to get right and the most work to maintain.

Jargon busting

Ball-to-target line or target line This is an imaginary line between your ball and your target.
Inside the line The side of the target line on which you stand.
Outside the line The opposite side of the line to which you stand.
Square This can refer to the club-face or to your body. Your club-face is square if it is aimed directly at the ball-to-target line. Your body is square when your shoulders, knees and toes are all aligned parallel to the ball-to-target line.
Open Club-face or body aims left of the target line.
Closed or shut Club-face or body aims right of the target line.

Aiming straight

1

To hit a straight shot, the club must be square at impact – it must be aiming straight at your target. So when you address the ball, the first thing you should do is set the club-face square to the target. Pick a point on your target line a few yards in front of the ball. Now square your club-face to this spot.

2

Now you have 'spot marked' the club-face accurately, build the rest of your stance around this alignment. You need to make your shoulders, hips, knees and toes all align parallel to the ball-to-target line. You are now aligned square.

Top tip

Establish good alignment by imagining you are playing golf on parallel train tracks. These tracks are running away from you in a completely straight line, your ball is on the far track and your feet on the near. This is how your alignment should be – shoulders, hips, knees and toes all parallel to the target line for a straight shot.

Practice drill
Clubs on ground

Any time you are hitting balls on the practice ground, you should work on your alignment. Place two clubs on the ground – one along your toes, the other parallel and just outside the target line. Every time you hit a shot, take a second to check you have aligned your body – from toes to shoulders – parallel to these two clubs. You can be working on your backswing or your pitching or anything but keep these clubs in place and keep checking to make it second nature.

Stance

Stance, as opposed to posture, is about the width of your feet and the ball position. Each club requires a slightly different stance – longer clubs need more stability in the stance.

Many beginners worry about how far away from the ball they should stand. Stand where you are comfortable, with your hands directly below your shoulders, dangling in a relaxed position. Also make sure that there is at least a hand's width between your thigh and the butt end of the club.

Here is an exercise to help you form a good stance for a driver. The stance will change for other clubs, but the driver is the least forgiving of all the weapons in your bag.

If you make a small mistake when addressing the ball, the driver will ruthlessly expose it.

Start by making your stance accurate for this club and the mid- and short-irons will seem much easier.

The perfect stance

1
Take your driver and tee up a ball. Stand with your feet close together with the ball opposite your left heel. Place the club-head behind the ball and check it is opposite your left heel.

2
Take your right foot back, leaving your left foot where it is. Stand so your feet are at least shoulder-width apart, with your heels underneath the points of your shoulders.

3
Point your toes outward slightly – the ball remains opposite your left heel, the perfect position for a driver.

Weight distribution at address

Driver address
Weight shift through a swing is vital. Your weight moves on to your right side in the backswing and on to the left through impact. Start well by having 60 per cent of your weight on your right side at address when hitting a driver as this makes you strike the ball on the sweeping upward part of the swing.

Iron address
With the shorter irons, as the ball comes back in your stance, your weight should be more evenly spread. You want to have a steeper angle of attack at impact, generating a slightly downward blow, as opposed to the sweeping, more shallow angle needed to hit woods.

Measuring stance width

The width of your stance is important for a decent swing; if your legs are too wide, you'll restrict your swing; too narrow and you'll lose control. To ensure you are not standing with your legs too far apart, use this measure.

Hold the end of a club in each hand and hang them from your shoulders as you take an address position. Let the clubs dangle freely and note where the clubs point. For longer irons and woods, the clubs should point at the inside of your heels.

The importance of ball position

The position of the ball in your stance may seem trivial, but those few centimetres can make a big difference. You must place the ball in a slightly different position for each club. For every single shot, whether it is a drive, a short-iron, a bunker shot or a putt, concentrate on ball position. It is easy to slip into bad habits and find the ball has moved in your stance for particular shots.

The basic rule for ball position is that the shorter the club, the more central the ball. You should hit a driver from opposite your left heel, as explained previously, play a 5-iron from just forward of centre and an 8-iron to wedge in the centre of your stance.

The ball position dictates at which point in your swing you make contact. The longer the club, the more shallow the swing – so you need to place the ball forward to sweep it off the turf or tee during the upward part of your swing.

Contact point

On shorter clubs, the angle of attack is more steep as you hit with a slightly descending blow, taking a larger divot, hitting the ball higher and with more backspin.

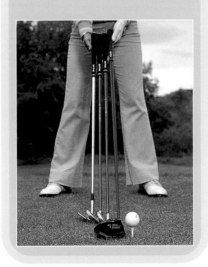

Ball position with a 3-wood

1
With a 3-wood, as above, the ball is forward in the stance, almost opposite the left heel. This tilts the left shoulder slightly higher than the right, angling the back away from the target in a strong position to sweep the ball off the deck.

2
The club makes contact in the upward part of the swing. The 3-wood approaches the ball from a shallow angle and sweeps it off the turf cleanly without taking a divot. The forward ball position makes this possible.

Ball position with a pitching-wedge

Jargon busting

Shallow swing This is when the club-head returns to the ball at impact level to the ground, hitting the ball on the upward part of the swing.

Steep swing The opposite of above, where the club hits down on the back of the ball from an acute angle, relative to the ground.

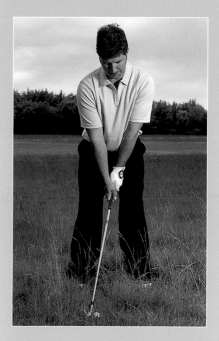

1

With a pitching-wedge, the ball is more central in the stance. Because of the ball position and the length of the shaft, you are set to strike the ball with a descending blow as opposed to a sweep.

2

The central ball position makes the club take a bigger divot as it hits down into the back of the ball, firing it higher into the air with greater backspin, which is what you need to stop the ball on the green.

When in trouble...

Whenever you find yourself in a tricky spot, whether it is in a bunker, in some thick rough or in a divot on the fairway, ball position can come to the rescue.

With all difficult lies, you want to strike the bottom of the ball. If the ball is near your right heel, this will make the swing steeper and you will attack it with a downward blow, driving to its bottom. So play the ball off your right foot to escape nasty lies.

Trouble-shooting: common faults

Erratic hitting, slices, hooks, duffs and thins can, more often than not, be traced to problems with your address position.

This is one of the most important elements of achieving a good golf swing. Ask any PGA professional and they will say that 90 per cent of problems in a golf swing start at the address. Develop solid fundamentals from the outset and you will save a fortune on golf lessons.

Here are four common mistakes at address, the resulting problems and hints on avoiding such difficulties.

Common errors Address

Ball too far back
If the ball is too far back in the stance when hitting with a long-iron or wood, this can lead to a number of problems, but it will be difficult to hit longer clubs consistently if the ball is too central. If you find you are topping (catching the top half of the ball) or fatting (hitting too much turf before the ball), check your ball position – it should be opposite your left heel.

Stance too narrow or too wide
If you find you are losing power or lack control with your swing, you may be standing with your feet too close together or too far apart. As a rule, they should be a shoulder-width apart – only with a driver can you widen this slightly. You will restrict your ability to turn in the swing if your stance is too wide and you will struggle to keep your balance if it is too narrow.

Weight favouring left side
The usual outcome of faulty weight distribution is weak shots. Power in the swing comes from weight transfer – your weight moves to your right side on the backswing and on to the left through impact – so starting with your weight on the right helps this initial movement. With a driver, place a little weight on your right at address – when playing shorter irons, spread it evenly across your feet and never place weight on your left when making a full swing.

Misalignment

Not only will you miss the target, but misalignment can affect the rest of your swing. Your natural instincts try to correct flaws in alignment leading to slices, hooks, pushes and pulls. To avoid misaligning, practise regularly with clubs on the ground. Start building your address by first aiming the club-face at the target, then making sure you have aligned your toes, knees, hips and, most crucially, your shoulders parallel to the target line.

Set-up checklist

Grip
- Back of left hand and palm of right facing target
- Grip in fingers, not palm of hands
- Relaxed grip with no tension

Ball position
- Opposite left heel for driver, central for wedge
- Comfortable distance from you and arms below shoulders

Posture
- Straight back, standing tall
- Flex in knees, chin off chest
- No slouching

Alignment
- Club-face square to target
- Shoulders, hips, knees and toes aligned parallel to target line

Weight
- Favouring right side at address with driver
- Evenly spread across stance with shorter clubs.

Mastering the basics of the set-up will help you develop a solid swing, and save you money on golf lessons.

The backswing

🕐 **1 hour**

🚩 **Goal** To develop a good technique to the top of the backswing

Difficulty rating ⚪⚪⚪⚫⚫
With good fundamentals, this should be simple, but it still needs work and understanding

The takeaway

If 80 per cent of problems in the swing come from address, a further 10 per cent come from a faulty first movement. Making a decent takeaway will set you on-course for a solid swing as it affects every movement that follows. This is the trigger for reaching a powerful and solid position at the top of the backswing.

Rhythm and timing

Many golfers become obsessed by positions in the swing and forget that the aim is to strike balls cleanly. A good rhythm and timing can overcome the imperfect swing so work on the basic technique and remember that this should be a natural, dynamic motion.

The stroke

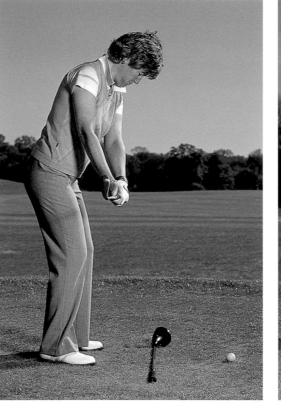

1
Be loose and relaxed as you take the club away. The club-head should remain on the target line in the first movement, so keep your posture and let your weight begin to move on to your right.

2
Think 'slow and low' as you swing away; take the club back smoothly with no jerks and try to keep it as low to the ground as you can.

Practice drill
Halfway back

If you have ever watched the 2003 Masters champion Mike Weir play, you will notice a quirk in his pre-shot routine. He swings the club halfway back, stops, then addresses the ball for real before hitting. He is checking his position halfway back – making sure he is on line.

Copy this practice to help your game. Place an extra club behind the ball on the target line. Start your takeaway, making sure your club-head stays on line and that you don't take it outside or inside. When your club reaches the horizontal, it should also be parallel to the club on the ground. When you get this right, stop and hit a ball while trying to replicate this position.

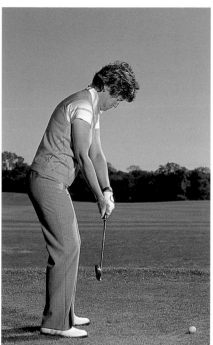

Taking the club outside
Avoid taking the club outside the line – that is, away from your body. This could cause problems at the top of your swing and may well result in problems with alignment, grip or posture, so keep a check on these basics.

Taking the club inside
The opposite of taking the club back outside the line is swinging too far on the inside. You will have difficulty with consistency if the club gets lost behind you. Keep the club-head in front of your body throughout the swing.

It's a funny old game

Many good golfers may have funny positions here but ability, experience and practice overcome these problems, so get it right initially and the rest of the swing will take shape naturally.

Jim Furyk, the 2003 US Open champion takes the club away on the outside but he has one of the most peculiar swings in world golf – he uses all his funny movements so he can compensate for this quirky position. He is also blessed with extraordinary natural timing and ability, which helps when hitting sweetly.

Wrist hinge

A source of great power in the swing comes from your wrists. If you hit the ball with rigid wrists, you are not only in danger of hurting your back, you will also struggle to find any distance, however strong you are. By hinging your wrists on the backswing, then rehinging them through impact, you create extra snap and a big increase in club-head speed.

Jargon busting

Club-head speed How fast your club-head travels as you hit the ball. The faster it travels, the further the ball flies.
Overswing When the club is swung too far in the backswing, causing a loss of power.

A perfect hinge

1
You must keep that width in the swing as you initially take the club away, but once your left arm is parallel to the ground, your wrists should hinge so that there is a solid right angle between the shaft and your left forearm.

2
This is as much wrist hinge as you need on the way back. From this position, you need to turn your shoulders to the top and there is no need to hinge your wrists any further. If you do, you will have to bend your arms, which will cause a loss in power – this is known as an overswing.

Common errors Backswing

Overswinging
This happens to golfers who have watched John Daly and think that the further back you swing, the further you will hit the ball. If you swing too far trying to hinge your wrists too much, your arms bend and you will struggle.

Not hinging enough
Similarly, if you have no wrist hinge, you will have no power. If the club shaft points skyward at the top of your backswing, you need more hinge, otherwise you will hit weak shots.

Left arm straight

Golf is a great game for advice and 'keep your left arm straight' is a common maxim, rooted in truth. Often though, golfers think it means your whole left arm, hands and all. This is wrong. Keeping your left arm straight at the top of the backswing is fine, but make sure you hinge your wrists as well, otherwise you will suffer powerless, wild shots.

1

To help develop the feel of wrist hinge, make practice swings by starting the club ahead of the ball at address, with your wrists turned over. Take a normal grip, but place the club-head a foot in front of the ball so that your right hand has come over the top of your left. Make sure your grip is loose.

2

Now swing to a halfway back position naturally, letting your wrists hinge. Starting with the club ahead of the ball adds momentum to the club-head and automatically sets your wrists in a good position on the backswing. Replicate this feeling when you are over the ball.

Like playing tennis

The best tennis players in the world boom big serves from a standing start: their shoulders and back coil then unleash and, as they hit the ball, their wrists snap, adding extra venom. Try throwing a ball without hinging your wrists and you'll not get too far. The same is true with a golf swing: your wrists add that extra energy needed to power the ball further down the fairway.

Rotation

To hit the ball powerfully and consistently, you need to hinge your wrists on the backswing and learn to rotate your body correctly, creating 'coil'. The more coil you produce, the more power you have.

As you swing back, rotate your upper body so that your back faces the target. As you turn your shoulders, keep the lower half of your body as still as you can – the difference between upper and lower body creates coil. This is called a shoulder turn. The difference creates resistance between your two halves, like a coiled spring, which unwinds on your downswing. Not everyone has the same flexibility, so don't worry if you can't turn your back fully to the target; keep the thought, turn as far as you can, and you'll be doing the right thing.

Rotation – where the top half of your body rotates leaving your bottom half still – creates the coil that provides you with more hitting power.

Practice drill **Rotation**

1
To practise a good turn, take up a normal address position as though you were about to strike the ball, concentrating on maintaining that good posture and balance – don't just flop over the ball. Cross your arms over your chest, resting them on your shoulders.

2
Now turn to the top of your backswing, keeping your height. Practise developing that coil by turning to the top while keeping your lower body still. Keep thinking: 'turn my back to the target.'

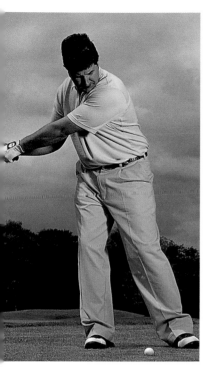

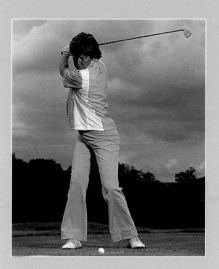

Not coiling

Golfers often know that they should shift their weight on the backswing and that they should turn their shoulders. With that thought in mind, they end up moving laterally, sliding their weight on to the right foot instead of coiling behind the ball.

Not rotating

As there is no turn in this position and the golfer's back is not facing the target, it is a weak position. The weight is on the right side, which is a good thing, but he has swayed into position and not rotated. His body has moved sideways and he has simply lifted his arms, rather than turning behind the ball.

Restricting head movement

This is probably the biggest myth in golf and causes the most problems. If you keep your head completely still, you will not be able to turn your shoulders fully. Your head has to move slightly, otherwise you will restrict your swing. You want to look at the ball through your left-eye at the top of the backswing and don't keep your head down at impact. US Tour star David Duval doesn't even look at the ball at impact as he knows this will restrict the full flourish of his swing.

Why some golfers hit it so far

There are many golfers who hit the ball miles while seeming to be the smallest in the pack. Look at Charles Howell III, the young US Tour pro. He weighs next to nothing and is not particularly tall, yet is one of the longest hitters in the world. This is because of his coil. He can turn his shoulders over 90° while keeping his lower body stable, turning it maybe 40°. The difference in lower and upper body is what produces the power as he winds up like a powerful spring before exploding through the ball. Flexibility leads to power.

Weight transfer

To create a powerful and consistent swing, you must make full use of all the assets you've been given. This means using your whole body to hit the ball, not just your hands and arms. To do this properly, you will need to have an effective weight transfer: your weight moves behind the ball on to the right side on the backswing, then through on to your left towards impact.

Correct weight transfer

Address

As always, getting things right in the swing means getting things right at address. Start as you mean to go on in the swing, with 60 per cent of your weight loaded on to your right foot at address. This will encourage a good shift in the first movement.

Halfway

Halfway back, you want your weight to have shifted mainly on to your right side. Don't overdo it; just feel your weight pressing on your right instep as you swing back. As with every movement in the swing, stay relaxed and under control.

Top

At the top of your swing, 80 per cent of your weight should be on your right foot, with only 20 per cent on your left. This may mean that your left heel lifts off the ground slightly, which is fine, especially if you are not hugely flexible, and your head will have moved. You are now well loaded for a powerful downswing where the weight transfers on to your left side and through the ball.

Common errors **Backswing**

Focus your thoughts...
'Slow and low' – this will trigger a series of smooth movements to the top.

'Turn back to the target' – this will encourage a good shoulder turn and coil, producing power in the swing.

Weight stuck on left side
A common problem with beginners is an incorrect weight transfer. Instead of your weight shifting on to your right as you swing back, your right leg straightens and your weight gets stuck on the left.

Leaning back
When you swing down and through, your weight has nowhere to go but backwards, shifting from your front foot towards your back. Your weight does not go through the ball and the result is a weak shot that can go anywhere, but which is rarely straight. This is known as a reverse pivot with the golfer leaning back in his finish position – a familiar sight on all golf courses.

Backswing checklist

● Take the club away slow and low
● Keep the club on line; don't take away outside or inside the line
● Wrists should be hinged when left arm is parallel
● Turn shoulders to the top, keeping wrist hinged
● Transfer 80 per cent of weight to your right foot by keeping flex in right knee.

It happens to the best of them

Jose Maria Olazabal has won two Masters titles while battling with the reverse pivot. It makes him struggle with his driver and woods, but when it comes to shorter irons, there are few better players in the world. Not everyone is blessed with his talent around the greens, though, so developing a good weight shift is vital.

The downswing

🕐 **45 minutes**

🚩 **Goal** To create a good transition and powerful impact position

Difficulty rating ● ● ○ ○ ○
Needs work and practice

The downswing should be as smooth and controlled as the backswing – maintain relaxed muscles and let a natural rhythm return the club-head to the ball.

Practice tip

Try this simple practice. Swing to the top of your backswing, then make a small pause, before starting your downswing. Feel like you are being lazy, as though you are putting no effort into the strike and the only force that's taking hold is gravity. This tiny pause, and it must only be a fraction of a second, gathers the moving parts of your swing and stops your arms starting the downswing.

The transition

1
This is the moment the swing starts down and you begin to return the club to the ball for impact. Often this is the critical part of the swing, which dictates whether you'll make a pure strike or not. You must start to shift your weight on to your left side at this point, while maintaining the tempo of your backswing.

2
Your downswing should start with your hips rotating left and triggering your upper body to uncoil, with your left shoulder moving away from your chin. If you start with your arms you may struggle to make a decent strike – the lower body starts the downswing and everything else follows.

Common errors Downswing

Top tip
A shorter swing creates more power and, in case you needed proof, look at the professionals. Tiger Woods worked on this after he had won the Masters in 1997 and discovered no loss of distance – just increased accuracy and lots more Major victories. Most high-handicap golfers would be better players if they shortened their swings.

Overswing

If you swing too far back and are trying to look like John Daly, your left arm will bend at the top. As you start the downswing, you will have to put energy into straightening that arm, energy that should go into the back of the ball. Almost all high-handicap golfers need to shorten their swings to keep that left arm straight at the top, which leads to a more consistent and more powerful downswing.

Starting with right shoulder

This is one of the most common problems in golf: starting down with your upper body and, more importantly, your right shoulder. It is a result of golfers becoming too aggressive and trying to hit the ball, rather than swing through it, and is known as 'coming over the top'. Almost all golfers who slice suffer from this problem. Try the 'headcover' drill to improve your transition.

Practice drill
Headcover

Place a headcover under your right armpit and make some practice swings. Keep the headcover in place to the top of your swing and then start down. If the cover drops as you start down, then you have come over the top and not started your transition effectively. Practise until you understand the feeling of keeping that right elbow close to your side on the downswing. Now hit practice balls trying to repeat this motion.

The hitting zone

The part of the swing that matters most is impact. If you are able to get the club-head square to the ball as it strikes, you will hit a straight shot. All your preparation, practice and technique works towards this one moment.

Although the moment of impact is the most important part of your swing, getting to this point means mastering the basics.

Halfway down

1

On the backswing, you hinged your wrists when your left arm was parallel to the ground. You want to retain that angle on your downswing until it naturally straightens at the ball. The longer you keep it, the faster the club will travel through impact – providing you are able to move your hands quickly enough.

2

It is inadvisable to try and physically keep this angle as you may end up blocking everything, but if you work on quickening your hands through the ball, you will increase your distance, so it is helpful to understand.

Weight check

Halfway down, your weight should move powerfully on to your left side. Imagine you are throwing a ball. You would wind up on to your back foot then move your weight on to your front as you fling. The same is true with the golf swing – you have wound up on to your right side and now you are delivering your powerful 'throw' by shifting on to your left.

Impact

1
There is no way to trick impact. Whatever you have done in your swing to this point, good or bad, will be found out. If everything has gone according to plan, you'll pierce your ball miles down the fairway and straight. If you had any problems at address, in your backswing or during your downswing – the ball will be out of control.

2
Keep your head slightly behind the ball at impact as you will find it tough to square the club if it gets ahead. Your hips will naturally move left as you strike, giving you room to free your arms and you should have at least 70 per cent of your weight on your left side.

Focus your thoughts...
Imagine that the ball is incidental to the swing; it is simply collected by your club, rather than actually being hit. This will help you swing smoothly through impact. Feel like the ball gets in the way of the swing.

The one part of the golf swing that is identical for everyone is the moment of impact. If you develop a technique with the odd eccentricity that works for you, don't worry – if it works, it works.

Impact checklist

- Head behind ball
- Wrists straightened at impact
- Weight on left side
- Left knee moves forward over front foot.

Practice drill
Impact position

If you practise hitting an impact bag or an old sofa-cushion, you can strengthen your position at impact. The cushion offers great resistance in comparison to a golf ball so when you whack it, your weight transfers more powerfully into it. This will also give you an indication of how good your position is as you make contact with the ball. If you are in a good position, you have a better chance of hitting a good shot.

Finishing off

Your finish position will be a reaction to how you swung the club although there are elements in your finish that can help your complete swing.

The release

Releasing the club is the result of your wrist hinge on your backswing. As you straighten your wrists through impact, they turn over just after you've hit the ball. If you don't manage this properly you will fire the ball weakly right.

This is a natural reaction to your earlier wrist hinge, but if you can try to create a mirror image in your follow-through, think 'hinge – rehinge' and your swing will have extra snap and power.

The extension

Fully extend your arms once you have struck the ball. If your arms bend on or just after impact, you will be lifting the club away from the ball as opposed to driving down the target line. The extension will only last a split second, but is a good thought to have.

Thinking to reach that full extension will stop you swinging too steeply into the back of the ball, helping you sweep through as opposed to hitting down. This will help transfer all the power you have created in the backswing through the ball.

The complete finish

Completing your swing in a controlled, balanced position means you have made a controlled and balanced swing. If you've cut across the ball or swung around your body, you will look ungainly and out of control, so the finish position is a good indicator of how you swung the club.

Aim for a good finish as you swing and this will help you accelerate through the ball. As your back faced the target at the top of the backswing, try to make your waist face the target in your finish. Let your head come up so you can watch where the ball finishes – don't get stuck looking at the ground – and your weight should now be almost entirely on your left foot.

Downswing checklist

- Transfer weight on to your left side as you start down
- Start downswing with your left hip
- Don't start with your right shoulder or arms
- Hold your wrist hinge on way down
- At impact, hips are open to target, weight is on left side and left knee is straight
- Release powerfully through impact and extending arms
- Make a full balanced finish.

Beware the stopped clock

A good finish position does reflect a good swing, but there are occasions where golfers manufacturer a wonderful finish, when they've got a rotten swing. This makes them look the part but does no good to their scorecard. It is fine looking great in one position, but remember the golf swing is a dynamic thing stuffed full of moving parts – one good point does not make a good swing. After all, even a stopped clock tells the right time twice a day.

End of Day 1: Key reminders

Day 1 is all about the fundamentals: grip, posture, set-up and alignment. These are the most crucial elements to get right if you are going to build a technically sound golf swing. If you are having trouble with your swing, more often than not you'll find the answer in your fundamentals. The actual swing is not as complicated as you might think, especially if you have good basics.

Here are key reminders for each of the four lessons you have been through in this section of this book. Use it as a reference tool when your technique goes awry as well as a careful reminder of what you've just learned.

Lesson 1: The grip

- Back of left hand, palm of right hand facing target
- Grip in fingers, not palm of hands
- Relaxed grip with no tension.

Lesson 2: The set-up
Ball position
- Opposite left heel (driver), central (wedge)
- Comfortable distance from you
Posture
- Straight back, standing tall, no slouching
- Flex in knees, chin off chest
Alignment
- Club-face square to the target
- Shoulders, hips, knees and toes aligned parallel to target line
Weight
- Favour right side with driver
- Evenly spread across stance with shorter clubs.

A good swing starts with a good position and technique at address – work hard on these.

The first movement must be smooth and slow, keeping the club on line for as long as possible.

At the top of the backswing, your weight should be on your right side with your shoulders turned 90°.

Lesson 3: The backswing

- Take the club away slow and low
- Keep the club on line; don't take away outside or inside the line
- Wrists should be hinged when left arm is parallel
- Turn shoulders to the top, keeping wrist hinged
- Transfer 80 per cent of weight on to your right foot by keeping flex in right knee.

Lesson 4: The downswing

- Transfer weight on to your left side as you start down
- Start downswing with your left hip
- Don't start with your right shoulder or arms
- Hold your wrist hinge on way down
- At impact, hips are open to target, weight is on left and left knee is straight
- Release powerfully through impact and extending arms
- Make a full balanced finish.

Instinctive flow

Although I have looked in detail at the movements involved in striking a golf ball, I must reiterate that swinging a club is a rhythmical motion. You must incorporate a certain amount of natural tempo, timing and feel as you strike. Without this you will have a staccato technique that may look good but is practically useless. Golf is more art and instinct than science and research. If you get too bogged down in technique, you will lose sight of this and play badly.

As you start down, move your weight through the ball on to your left, keeping the swing smooth.

The moment of truth – impact. All you need is your club-head to be square to the target as you strike.

A swing is a rhythmical, natural and instinctive movement – keep it that way by keeping it simple.

Day 2

Game development

Holding the club correctly, addressing the ball accurately and developing a full, consistent swing is the basis of any golf technique. This is only one aspect of the game, however. To become a decent or even respectable golfer, you must be confident in the other aspects of the sport.

Most of the techniques and tips you will learn in Day 2 share the same fundamentals as the full swing. When pitching or hitting fairway bunker shots, you still hold the club in the same way and you still want to keep strong posture. The goals of the second day are to introduce other techniques: how to putt consistently; how to chip and pitch around the green; how to escape the dreaded bunkers; and what to do when you're faced with thick rough or nasty lies – everyday situations on the golf course.

By the end of Day 2, you will be familiar with all the terms and jargon of the business end of golf, where you can make your scores count and begin to enjoy the competitive side of the sport. Short-game and trouble shots can bring as much discontent as joy. Many golfers find it easier to hit the ball closer from 137m (150yd) than 9m (20yd), which seems strange. As always, problems often come from faulty fundamentals, so get these right from the outset and golf becomes a whole lot easier.

Jargon busting

Pin A flag marking where the hole is cut.
Fringe Slightly longer grass around the edge of the green.
Bunker A crater-like depression in the ground filled with sand designed to catch your ball. They may be placed around the green or on the edge of fairways.
Rough Long grass that encircles the fairways and greens.
Semi-rough An area between the fairway and rough, where the grass is longer than the fairway but shorter than the rough.
Lie This describes how the ball sits on the ground. Do you have a good or bad lie?

Pitching and chipping

⏱ **1 hour**

🚩 **Goal** To develop good pitching and chipping techniques and to learn when to use them

Difficulty rating ⚪⚫⚫⚫⚪
Work and practice needed to develop consistency

Pitching and chipping are vital in holding a score together and keeping your handicap down. When you are around the green, being able to hit the ball close and one-putt regularly is the difference between high- and low-handicap golfers. This is also the most creative part of the game, where imagination, touch and feel are as important as a good swing.

Jargon busting

The up-and-down You will often hear golfers and commentators talking about 'up-and-downs'. This is a term used for chipping, pitching and bunker play. An up-and-down is when you chip or pitch and only take one putt to hole out. Usually, you have hit the ball dead and left yourself a small putt. Good golfers will have consistent up-and-downs, rarely needing two putts after a chip or pitch.

Pitching **The grip**

Grip for the pitch shot
A pitch tends to be over a longer distance than a chip, although this is not always the case (see page 63). The ball will fly further through the air, landing gently and stopping quickly.

Use your orthodox grip for the pitch shot, but grip down the shaft. This will give you more control of the club-head and improve your feel and touch for the shot. Usually you pitch with a pitching-wedge, but if you need to play a shot that will fly higher and stop quicker, use either a sand- or lob-wedge.

Hold the club gently; you do not want tension in your arms. They need to feel relaxed, loose and fluid to help with touch and feel. A pitch is not as mechanical as a full-shot – it is more about instinct and natural flair.

Pitching The set-up

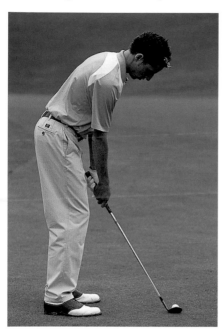

Common error Pitching

Dos and Don'ts

Do
- ✔ Choke down the grip
- ✔ Hold the club gently
- ✔ Align your body left of the target
- ✔ Place the ball back in your stance
- ✔ Touch the club gently on the ground

Don't
- ✘ Grab hold of the club tightly
- ✘ Stand with your feet a shoulder-width apart
- ✘ Align parallel to the target
- ✘ Have a central ball position.

1
For a pitch, you want to aim slightly left of the target, giving your arms space to swing through the ball. Through the swing you will not be moving the lower half of your body too much and aiming left will help with this. Keep the club square to the target. A good tip is to rest the club gently on the grass, or hover it slightly off the ground; this helps to release the tension in the grip and will improve your feel for this shot.

2
When pitching, you want to hit down on the back of the ball, making a crisp clean strike to give you the greatest amount of control. Place the ball back in your stance and push your hands forward at address to help with this. The ball should be opposite your right heel. Make sure you are standing with your feet closer together than for a normal, full swing. A narrow stance will stop you using your lower body, ideal in a pitch.

Poor address position
Often at address, golfers will stand to the ball with a normal address position, with their legs a shoulder-width apart and the ball central in the stance. You will have too much lower body movement if you adopt this posture, which will make it very difficult to strike the ball consistently and to control it on the putting surface. You mustn't align parallel to the target either; make sure you are aiming slightly left at address.

Wedge checkpoint

Look at any decent player's bag and they will have at least three wedges, if not four. To add to your versatility around the greens, increase the number of wedges in your bag. A standard set will come with a pitching- and sand-wedge. By adding a club that is more lofted than a sand-wedge, usually called a lob-wedge, you will be able to play a greater variety of shots. With more loft, you can fly the ball higher in the air, while making it land softly, useful when you are pitching to a pin cut close to bunker or water.

Pitching **The swing**

1
Once you have taken that good address position, you are in a good shape to make a solid swing. This is an 'arms and shoulders' swing; keep the lower body still and quiet, controlling the club with your upper body.

2
The swing is a simple 'back and through' motion; you take the club back with your arms, rotating your upper body so that your back faces the target. The backswing determines how far you will hit the ball. To hit further, take a longer backswing; do not take the club as far back to hit a shorter pitch. When your hands reach waist height, you want to hinge your wrists so the club is at 90° to your arms.

3
From this position in your backswing, you want to think 'through', rotating your body so it faces the target, catching the ball on the way. Swing through the ball positively; you must accelerate through impact as deceleration is the cause of most disastrous pitches. Keep the rhythm in your swing the same for every pitch shot – just vary the length of the backswing for different distances.

4
Your hands finish an equal distance through the shot as they did on the backswing. This will help you swing through the ball aggressively, with a solid, tight technique. Aiming to finish in a good natural position will help your natural feel and touch for the shot.

Common error **Pitching**

Decelerating towards impact
The biggest mistake when pitching is decelerating towards impact. Slowing your stroke on the downswing will destroy your rhythm and will lead to either catching the ball halfway up, firing low and too far (a thin); or catching the turf before the ball, trundling it a few yards forward. The key is to keep your rhythm and pace of swing consistent, but to vary the length of your backswing for the length of the shot.

Dos and Don'ts

Do
✔ Control the length of the shot with the length of your backswing
✔ Hinge your wrists to 90° once they reach waist height
✔ Rotate your back so it faces the target on the backswing
✔ Swing positively through, accelerating towards impact
✔ Concentrate on a positive, tight finish, swinging your hands as far through as back

Don't
✘ Use excessive amounts of lower body in the swing
✘ Keep your wrists straight through the shot
✘ Swing with your arms alone and not your upper body
✘ Decelerate towards impact
✘ Concentrate on keeping your head down as this will destroy the flow of the swing.

Even the best golfers in the world will miss a smattering of greens with their approach shots over 18 holes. This means that to keep a score going, they have to chip well, with confidence and consistency. This is the business end of the game, where you hold a score together and take pressure off other parts of your game.

Jargon busting

Chip-in Holing a chip shot.
Chip-and-run Chip shot that rolls most of the way to the hole.
Lob Where the ball flies most of the way to the hole.
Release After the ball has bounced it 'releases' to the hole.

Chipping **The set-up**

Chipping well keeps a good score going and rescues a bad one. If you can chip well, it will take the pressure off other parts of the game.

1
Like a pitch shot, a chip is easier to play if you open your stance at address – align your body slightly left of the target. Keep around 60 per cent of your weight on your right side and aim the club-face at the target. Don't grab the club too hard, but choke down the grip to give yourself better control of the club-head.

2
The shaft of the club and your left arm should form a straight line with your hands forward of the ball. Place the ball back in your stance, so it is again opposite your right heel. Stand closer than you would for a pitch. Keep your stance narrow, which keeps your lower body still through the stroke.

The difference between a pitch and chip

The difference between these two shots is not, as many golfers think, the distances involved: that you chip from close, pitch from further away. This is not always accurate. You may find yourself playing a chip-and-run from 45m (50yd) on a hard-running links, yet you could be hitting an accurate pitch to a soft green from 30m (33yd). With a chip, the hands do not go higher than your hips. In a pitch, the hands pass your hips with wrist hinge. It is important to make the distinction, as it sets the framework for the shot, so you have full confidence with the swing you are using and will not hesitate in the stroke.

Weight rooted to left
Problems at address often come from misconceived good advice. You are meant to have your weight on your left side at address, but not at the exclusion of good balance and strong posture. Make sure that your weight favours the left, rather than being rooted on it, restricting movement in your shoulders and leading to a hands-led stroke.

Setting up too parallel
Do not set up too parallel to the ball-to-target line, otherwise you will find you miss the hole right, regularly. You want to open your stance slightly, and pull your left foot back to make room to swing down your toe line. Similarly, do not open up too much or you will find it difficult to make a consistent strike as you cut across the ball. You want to give your swing more space by aligning left, but do not overdo it.

Chipping **The swing**

1

If you have taken up a good address position then you are in good shape for a solid strike. Remember to get comfortable over the ball – this is a feel shot that requires imagination; it is difficult to have a good touch if you are feeling awkward.

2

Swing from your shoulders, taking the club straight back along your toe line. You have pre-set a good position at address so you want to keep the angle between the shaft and your forearms throughout the shot. Don't let the club-head get ahead of your hands at any point in the swing.

3

You are looking to return to your address position at impact. The length of your backswing determines the pace of the shot – the further you take the club back, the further the ball flies – and the loft of the club-face will lift the ball in the air.

4

Swing to a solid position, holding the club-face behind your hands as long as possible. You want to drive your left forearm towards the target as you accelerate through the ball to ensure a crisp strike.

Common errors Chipping

Top tip
You can chip with almost any club. When you are selecting a club to chip with, think which club would get the ball rolling on the putting surface as quickly as possible and use that club – it may be a 7- or 6-iron; you don't always have to use a pitching-wedge.

Lifting the ball with hands
A common problem is golfers trying to lift the ball into the air with their hands, instead of letting the club-head do the work. They will then break their wrists through the shot when they should be holding their wrists firm, causing the ball to thin through the back of the green. This is a swing that comes from your shoulders with relatively quiet hands – too much wrist can cause problems.

Decelerating towards impact
The biggest problem when chipping is deceleration. As soon as you hesitate in your stroke and slow down towards impact, your rhythm breaks, you lose the connection between your hands and shoulders, causing either a chunk (too much turf and not enough ball) or blade (too much ball not enough turf). Be bold with chips and accelerate the club-head towards impact for a sure strike.

Dos and Don'ts

Do
✔ Control the length of the shot with the length of your backswing
✔ Keep your wrists firm through the shot
✔ Return to your address position at impact
✔ Swing positively through, accelerating towards impact

Don't
✘ Use your wrists in the shot too much
✘ Let the club-head get ahead of the hands in the swing
✘ Use your lower body too much in the swing
✘ Decelerate towards impact.

Practice drills

To sharpen your short game, you need to get down to the practice green and play around with your chipping. Chipping is a fun, imaginative part of the sport where you can experiment and develop good technique. Here is a variety of drills that you can add to your practice routine to help develop:

- Technique
- Feel
- Imagination
- Confidence.

Technique: left wrist firm

To keep your technique solid and to stop you flicking at the ball with your wrists through impact, try this simple and effective drill. Put a comb or

pencil down the back of your glove on your left hand, so it runs up your left wrist and acts like a splint, stiffening your joints.

Now take some practice shots with the pencil in place. If you try to break your wrists, the pencil or comb will either dig into you slightly or make it

Feel: throw the ball

A great way to develop consistent feel is to throw the ball. Drop your club and lob, underarm, a series of balls at a target. You'll be surprised at how accurate you can be. We all have in-built, natural feel; if you lob a ball to someone to catch, you don't fling it way past their head or drop it on their toes. So by lobbing golf balls at a target it will give you a sense of your natural touch. Now stand over a chip and imagine you are going to lob the ball at the target. How hard will you hit it? Apply this feeling to your chipping stroke.

Imagination: chip with one ball only

1 Go to a green with one ball and a selection of clubs from a pitching-wedge to a 5-iron.
2 Chip the ball at the hole using the most lofted club – pay attention to its reaction on the green and make a mental note.
3 Pick the ball up and chip with the next lofted club.
4 Keep going until you have played a shot with every club, bearing in mind each club's reaction. By playing only one ball, you will concentrate on how it reacts and learn the different spins and rolls you achieve from each club.

difficult to straighten. By preventing this excessive hinge as you strike the ball, you will have a crisper, more consistent strike as a result.

Confidence: aim for landing areas

If you are struggling with feel and confidence, place three or four headcovers or bag towels around the green. Chip to each of those in turn, but use them as landing zones; not finishing targets. The more you concentrate on landing the ball in the right place, the less result-obsessed you will become. This will help you develop confidence over chip shots.

The chip putt

When you are just off the green and need to have a small amount of loft on the ball before it reaches the putting surface, try this technique.

1 Take a 7- or 6-iron and make a putting grip.
2 Set up to the ball as though you are about to hit a putt.
3 Use your putting stroke to strike the ball.

The shot is essentially a putt with a lofted club. It will give you great control for those shorter chip shots, around 9m (10yd), where you simply need to get the ball out, over the fringe and rolling as quickly as possible.

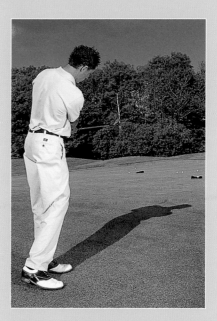

Land on flat parts of the green

As soon as you've struck the ball, you can't do anything about the outcome. You can allow for bad bounces, however, by aiming to land the ball on the flattest part of the green. If you have an unlucky kick, it will not be as disastrous and if you have a good bounce, it could end very close. So when you make your club selection, bear in mind the rub of the green and select a club that will put the odds in your favour.

Bunkers

90 minutes

| **Goal** To build an understanding of greenside and fairway bunker shots

Difficulty rating 🥚🥚🥚⚪⚪
Fear factor to be overcome, then it's a breeze

Playing out of bunkers and the rough is a common part of the beginner's game. Both hazards are troublesome but neither are unconquerable. Dealing with the tough spots is a crucial part of the game, so start with the easiest trouble shot of them all – the greenside bunker.

Greenside bunkers – the grip

Use either a sand-wedge or lob-wedge for a splash out of a greenside bunker as they are specifically designed for this surface. Take a normal grip on the club, but open the club-face slightly, so it will aim right of the target were you to set up normally.

Bunkers **The set-up**

1
With the club set slightly open, align your feet, shoulders and knees left of the target. In doing this, the club-face should aim straight at the target, which is most likely to be the pin.

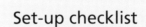

2
Shuffle your feet into the sand to find a firm base for the swing. This will also give you an idea of the texture of the sand. Flex your knees more than usual, so you feel like you are sitting more in the stance. Keep the ball forward and hover the club above the sand (it is against the Rules to ground your club in the bunker – see page 12).

Set-up checklist

● Open club-face, then take grip
● Align body left of target
● Square club-face to target
● Shuffle feet into sand
● Ball forward in stance and hover club.

Rules check

1
Having made these adjustments at address, you are set for a good bunker shot. Swing down the line of your body and not towards the target. Imagine a line along your toes; you want to take the club back along this line to the top of your backswing. Keep your backswing relatively short, let your wrists hinge and keep your arms loose – any stiffness or tension in your swing will cause problems.

2
Aim to swing aggressively through the sand, with the club-head entering the hazard slightly behind the ball. The design of the club and the adjustments you made at address will splash a handful of sand out of the bunker, bringing the ball out with it. You don't want the club to dig into the sand, but to skip through it, taking ball and sand on its way.

3
It is vital to accelerate through the ball and if you aim to have a strong full finish, this will help. Don't dig into the sand and leave the club there, but work on splashing through it to a strong finish position.

A bunker is deemed a hazard in the Rules of golf and water is another. Hazards are governed by peculiar rules. Your club is not allowed to touch the sand or water (known as grounding) before you play the shot or you will suffer a one-shot penalty.

Bunker tactics

1 The golden rule of bunker play is to make sure you only take one shot in the hazard. This may mean hitting out sideways or splashing away from the flag, to give yourself a chance of getting close with your next shot.

2 If you are able to attempt getting close, don't pick the hole as your target, choose the top of the flag; look to land the ball right on the pin. This will help you accelerate through the ball and will compensate for the sand slowing down the club-head and shortening the shot.

Practice drill **Circle in the sand**

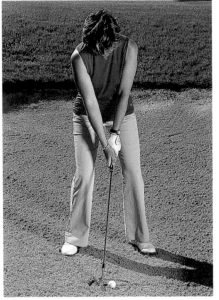

1
To help your confidence and to build a feel for a good bunker shot, drop a ball in the sand and draw a small circle around it with your finger. This is the amount of sand you should take with a greenside bunker shot.

2
Concentrate on hitting through the circle in the sand. There is no need to hit the ball at all; you simply lift that circle's sand out of the bunker, taking the ball with it. The ball floats out on a cushion of sand and will drop softly on the green.

Practice drill **Line of balls**   Common errors **Bunkers**

1
Draw a line in the sand at a right-angle to the ball-to-target line and place six balls 5cm (2 inches) in front of this line. Leave enough space between each ball. Set up to the first ball in the line.

2
You want to hit the line, which will lift the ball out of the bunker. Move down the line, hitting all the balls. Accelerate through the ball and you will become consistent and confident out of a bunker.

Closed club-face at impact
Taking your grip then opening the club-face. You must first open the club-face, then take your grip – doing it the other way round leads to a closed club-face at impact.

Not hitting along body line
Hitting at the target and not along your body line. You align left of the target and must swing down your body line, not at your target. The open club-face will make the ball fly straight.

Decelerating towards impact
If you hesitate in your swing, slowing on your downswing, you will either catch too much sand and leave the ball in the trap, or catch too much ball and thin it through the green. Always accelerate positively and smoothly to a full finish.

Using the right club

A common problem with golfers is using the wrong club to escape from the sand. Often, high-handicap golfers steer clear of the sand-wedge, which is an error – the sand-wedge is designed to make it one of the simplest clubs to use once your technique is right. The club has added 'bounce'; this is the wide part of metal on the club-head behind the leading edge. This 'bounce' makes the club skip through the sand like an ice-cream scoop, collecting sand and ball.

Fairway bunkers

A few set-up alterations, some sensible club selection and tactics will banish any fairway bunker demons. At first glance, that 135-metre (150-yard) plus bunker shot may seem impossible, but use this advice and surprise yourself.

Fairway bunkers **The set-up**

1
The aim of this shot is to catch the ball cleanly, taking as little sand as possible. The more sand you take, the less energy will be transferred to the ball. Try to hit the balls slightly thin as opposed to taking a divot. Grip the club more tightly – this helps you to catch the ball thin.

2
Grip down the shaft at address and have your feet slightly closer together. Place the ball a touch back in your stance and don't shuffle your feet into the sand. This set-up will keep your body still through the swing, which will help you catch the ball cleanly off the top of the sand.

Fairway bunker tactics

Assess the situation and evaluate your goals for the shot. Can you realistically clear the water in front of the green and fly the ball to the pin near the bunker? Probably not. Will a 5-iron really clear the lip of the bunker? Not often. Use these rules to make the right decision from a fairway trap.

1 The goal of all bunker shots is to escape in one shot – make this the priority.
2 Take one club longer than you would for this distance from the fairway.
3 Has this club got enough loft to escape the lip of the bunker? If not, make sure you use a club that will get you out.
4 How much will you gain from taking a risk and hitting it as far down the fairway as possible? Often it is easier to play from 90m (100yd) out than an awkward 45m (50yd).

Fairway bunkers **The swing**

1

Just as you take the club back, imagine you are playing from a thin pane of glass stretched over a 6-metre (20-foot) drop. You are balancing carefully on it and must not move your feet too much or catch the glass beneath the ball, otherwise the glass will break and you will fall.

2

The swing is a 'quiet' swing; you are striking the ball with an energetic upper body, but a still lower body. This will lose you distance, which is why you need to take the extra club. You want to make as little contact with the sand as possible.

3

You may feel ungainly in your follow-through but if you keep your lower body quiet and swing smoothly with your upper half, you will catch the ball cleanly. The longer club will carry the ball the distance you lose. Disturb as few grains of sand underneath the ball as possible.

Dos and Don'ts

Do

✔ Grip down the club
✔ Hold the club tighter
✔ Have your feet closer together
✔ Take an extra club for the distance
✔ Try to catch the ball slightly thin

Don't

✘ Shuffle your feet into the sand
✘ Use too little loft to escape the lip
✘ Use your lower body in the shot
✘ Take a divot.

Trouble shots

⏰ ⏰ **2 hours**

🚩 **Goal** To develop techniques for escaping difficult spots

Difficulty rating ●●●●○
Learn your limits and escape sensibly

Difficult lies

There are times in golf when you will crunch a drive 225m (250yd), splitting the fairway, only to find it sitting in an old divot that someone has not replaced. Either that or it is stuck in a tuft of grass or has a clump of mud plastered to the side. Worse still is when you hit the ball into a bunker and discover that the ball has plugged into the sand, looking like a fried egg with only the top visible. For all these trouble shots, the answers are the same; make simple set-up alterations and swing positively.

The trouble set-up

1
For most tough lies, the set-up changes you make are the same because the principles are the same – you need somehow to get the club-head at the ball despite encircling foliage and turf. First choke down the grip slightly and use a club with enough loft.

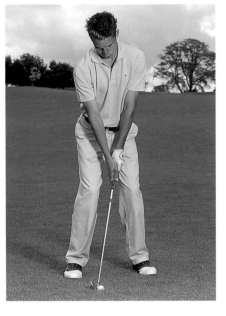

2
Place the ball back in your stance and move your hands forward slightly. This will promote a V-shape swing, which is good for attacking the ball steeply and getting it out of a tough spot. Use these set-up changes as a stock trouble-saving technique.

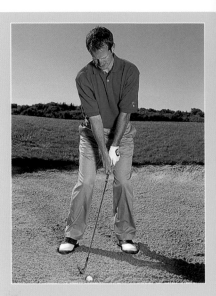

Plugged lie in bunker

Unlike an ordinary bunker shot, you will need to dig down into the sand to the bottom of the ball. Instead of opening your club-face, close it. Align your feet to the target and put the ball back in your stance. You need to chop down the back of the ball with the club-head, like a woodcutter chopping logs. Don't worry about the follow-through, just swing hard to the bottom of the ball. When it emerges, it will have no spin and will run through the green more, so be aware of this.

Hitting from a divot

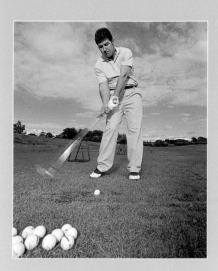

Practise trouble shots

Golfers curse their luck whenever they land in a tricky spot – a divot, an uphill lie, getting plugged in a bunker – but they are ignoring the most famous maxim in golf coined by South African legend Gary Player: 'the more I practise, the luckier I get'. Get out on the practice range, find a spot with some nasty divots and hit out of them. Plug some balls in a practice bunker and experiment with various escape shots. Find a sloping lie on the edge of a fairway and hit balls until you've worked out how they react. You will learn to develop surprising consistency from these positions.

1
Hitting from a divot is similar to hitting from any number of tricky spots where the ball sits down in a tough lie. Once you have made the set-up changes, you are looking to swing with controlled aggression; be powerful but not at the expense of rhythm and technique. Pick the club up steeply and hinge your wrists early in the stroke.

2
Hit down into the back of the ball. You are looking to take a divot within the divot; but keep your tempo. Your hands stay ahead of the club-head throughout the swing and you need to keep your wrists firm throughout the shot.

3
The follow-through will be short, as you will keep your wrists firm through impact and will catch a lot of turf as you dig to the bottom of the ball. You may find the ball slides from left to right in this shot, so aim slightly left of the target at address.

Coping with trouble spots

Golf is a game of decisions and playing from tricky spots is where your decision-making skills are tested to the limit. The rough is a varied and awkward place – you need the right tools and experience to escape. When you are stuck in a forest, there are some sensible measures you can take to resurrect your score.

These tips will help you make the right decision when you find yourself in an awkward situation. It could make the difference between wrecking your card and holding a match together.

Playing from the rough

1
If you have finished in the rough, you need to establish how far you can move the ball forward. You may be able to reach the green, but if you can't, it is not always sensible to hack as far down the fairway as possible. Try to leave yourself a distance with which you feel most comfortable. If your lie is awful, place the ball back in your stance; keep it central if the lie is okay.

2
You never get as much spin from the rough as you do from a good lie on the fairway. This is because grass becomes trapped between the grooves on your club and the ball. The grooves create spin, so without their contact, the ball flies further in the air and runs once it hits the ground. Be aware of this, especially if there is a clear run through to the flag from your position in the rough – you may be able to work the ball closer than you first thought.

3
Your set-up changes will make you swing more steeply into the back of the ball – the tougher the lie, the steeper the swing. You may need to add extra muscle to make sure the club-head does not get entangled in the rough, dragging the ball left. As with all trouble shots, don't worry about a photo finish. Simply swing aggressively.

The hockey shot – rescue tool

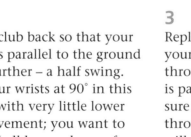

1

When you are in the trees or stuck for a clear shot to the green, the hockey shot is a great rescue tool for knocking the ball into play. Put the ball back in your stance a touch, have your feet close together and grip down a 6- or 7-iron. You are looking to hit a punch-shot low to a position of safety on the fairway.

2

Take the club back so that your left arm is parallel to the ground and no further – a half swing. Hinge your wrists at 90° in this position with very little lower body movement; you want to keep the ball low and away from overhanging branches or foliage.

3

Replicate your backswing with your finish position by swinging through so that your right arm is parallel to the ground. Make sure you accelerate aggressively through impact, otherwise you will catch the ball heavy and leave it in the rough.

Trouble rules

7/10 Rule When you are eyeing up a Seve Ballesteros-esque escape shot, stop. Think about the shot you are attempting – is it really within your ability to shape a ball 180m (200yd) around a large oak tree from the thick rough? If you think you could pull off such a shot seven times out of ten, then go ahead. If the odds are less, chip out sideways.

Magic 135m (150yd) When you need to escape trouble and are forced to lay up, don't take the high-risk club that will get you 18m (20yd) nearer the green if you are lucky. Instead, look for the 135m (150yd) markers instead. Once you are within the markers, you have a chance of hitting it close and taking one or most likely two putts but no worse.

Hitting from slopes

Here is a quick guide on how to play from slopes on the golf course. It is rare to find a completely flat lie on certain types of courses – links for example – so understanding the adjustments you have to make under those circumstances is crucial.

Slopes are not the terrifying things you might at first imagine, but are easily conquerable with simple set-up changes and swing thoughts. Once you have learned to understand how the lie of the land affects your ball flight, you can use it to your advantage by shaping it around obstacles and into tight pin positions. One thing is certain, if you fight the slope you are sunk. Always play with Mother Nature – not against her.

Ball below feet

The set-up

This is one of the more difficult shots in golf. Grip up the club and work to be comfortable at address. Flex your knees and widen your stance for improved balance.

The swing

1 The slope makes your swing more upright, which puts slice-spin on the ball, taking it right, so aim left of the target to compensate. Let your arms do the work in the backswing.

2 Don't worry about losing your balance after impact and trotting down the hill, but concentrate on keeping a smooth, even tempo until this point.

Uphill lies

The set-up

An uphill lie will add loft to your club, so take an extra club for that distance. The spine is at right angles and shoulders are as parallel to the slope as possible. Let your weight sit on your right foot.

The swing

1 Keep your swing short to retain balance and let your weight sit on your right knee on the backswing.

2 Feel like you are sweeping the ball up the slope through impact to your finish and try to not take a divot – pick the ball off the turf cleanly.

Ball above feet

The set-up
When the ball is above your feet, the slope is going to put draw-spin on the ball, which will make it curl left. So to compensate for this, aim right of your target. Grip down the club and stand tall to the ball.

The swing
1 Now swing as naturally as possible – all these troublesome shots involve set-up alterations followed by as normal a swing as possible. Swing shorter and don't fight the slope.

2 Maintain your balance through to your finish and beware that the ball will travel further from this lie. A draw-spin kills backspin, so it is wise to club down.

Downhill lies

The set-up
Place the ball back in your stance slightly and take a club with less loft, as the slope decreases the loft. Drop your left shoulder and keep your back at right-angles to the slope.

The swing
1 This is not an easy shot, so pick up the club steeply but maintain your tempo and rhythm. Keep your weight evenly spread throughout the swing and don't fight the slope.

2 You are looking to chase the ball down the slope; don't lean back to try and lift the ball in the air. Think that you are moving your hands down the hill as you swing.

Trouble spot checklist

Ball below feet
- Aim left of target
- Flex knees
- Maintain tempo

Uphill lies
- Take extra club
- Shoulders parallel to slope
- Catch ball cleanly

Ball above feet
- Aim right of target
- Take less club
- Choke down grip

Downhill lies
- Take less club
- Ball back in stance
- Hands swing down the slope.

Putting

🕐 🕐 **2 hours**

🚩 **Goal** To work on good putting fundamentals and a consistent stroke

Difficulty rating ⚪⚪⚪⚪⚪
A simple stroke, but a frustrating part of the game

Putting is more art than science. There are basic techniques but it is a part of the game that allows for peculiarities – for individual methods – more than most. When it comes down to it, putting is about feeling comfortable. A good grip and posture will help with this, but you will never putt consistently if you feel uncomfortable over the ball. If you look at the top golfers, their techniques, from grip to stroke, share fundamental similarities. The first thing to work on in putting is the grip.

Jargon busting

Break or borrow The slopes on the green that will affect your ball.
Reading the green To putt accurately you need to 'read' the break and borrow on the green.

Putting **The grip**

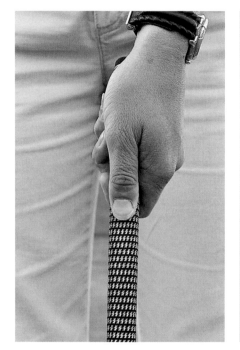

1
The aim of a good putting grip is to make the hands act as one – as a unit. Unlike the full swing where wrist hinge and hands are important for power and control, for the putting stroke you want to rely entirely on your shoulders and your grip must reflect this. The most common grip is the reverse overlap; place your left hand on the club first with the grip running through your palm.

2
Now place the right hand below the left, but make sure the palms of your hands face each other. Place your left index finger on top of the fingers of your right hand and keep both your thumbs on top of the centre of the grip. Shuffle your hands about so this is comfortable and your hands feel as one on the grip.

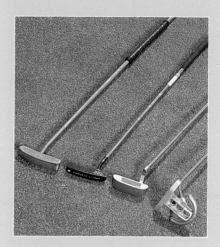

Using the right putter

The right putter for you will not be the right putter for someone else, or even anyone else, irrespective of the name printed on the back or its price-tag. Stick with what feels good. There is one proviso though: make sure your putter is the right length for your stroke – don't let your stroke fit the putter. A putter that is too long or too short will breed inconsistency.

1

Good posture at address is as important for putting as it is for your full swing. The address position is not too different from that for your full-shot. Your hands should hang naturally below your shoulders; you should have some flex in your knees, but not too much; and bend from the hips keeping your back straight.

2

Your feet should not be too wide apart; you will find it easier to keep your lower half still in the stroke if your feet are just under a shoulder-width apart. Play the ball a touch forward in your stance. To check ball position, take an address, drop a ball from your left eye and where it lands is a good ball position.

The putting stroke

The putting stroke should be one of the most simple to master in golf. You are not trying to hit the ball into the air, you are simply rolling it into a hole along the ground with minimal movement of your body – easy.

As with the rest of the swing, putting is a natural and fluid motion. As soon as you make the technique over complicated you will struggle to putt consistently. Always look to keep a natural element in your stroke, or you will never master the greens.

Putting time

Don't spend hours lining up putts and reading greens. If you take too long, you will make putting less instinctive – you must not over-analyze a putt or your stroke. Lee Trevino once explained: 'If you are going to miss a putt, miss it quickly.'

Putting **The basic stroke**

1
The key to putting consistently is to take your hands out of the stroke. You are looking to putt using your shoulders, which cannot do much except rock back and forward. At address, you will create a 'Y' between the club and your forearms. You want to keep this 'Y' in place throughout.

2
Take the club back and through straight – like a pendulum. Rock your shoulders back and keep your head completely still. You don't want to move any other part of your body except your shoulders.

3

At impact, catch the ball on the up-part of your swing. This will help roll the ball end over end, producing a more accurate roll across the putting surface. Keep your lower body as completely still as possible. Most mishit putts come from too much movement in legs and hips in the swing. There is no weight transfer in the putting stroke and no lower body movement.

4

Swing the putterhead through impact, so the ball gets in the way of the stroke as you accelerate to a positive finish. Any hesitation and deceleration leads to a bad putt. Hold your finish position for a few seconds once you have struck the ball and keep your eyes looking at the grass until the ball is well on its way to the hole. This will ensure you don't look up too early, moving your lower body and causing a mishit.

Focus your thoughts...

The 'Y' you create at address should be there throughout your entire stroke. Concentrate on holding it in place, only moving your shoulders through the stroke. This will create consistency and confidence in your stroke.

Be a grandfather clock. In a grandfather clock, the pendulum swings but the case does not move. When you are putting, the grandfather case is your body and the pendulum your shoulders, arms and putter. Only move the pendulum and keep the case completely still.

Dos and Don'ts

Do

✔ Hold the club gently
✔ Place it under your left eye
✔ Be comfortable over the ball
✔ Have a putter that suits your stroke
✔ Rock only your shoulders in the stroke

Don't

✘ Move your lower body in the stroke
✘ Use your wrists as you putt
✘ Move your head through the stroke
✘ Decelerate the club-head towards impact.

Long putts

Getting the ball close regularly when you are faced with a long putt is crucial to scoring well. If you can knock it dead with confidence from 6m (20ft) and further away, you will keep the score going and some are bound to drop for birdies.

Pace not line

The key to leaving yourself a short second putt is to judge the pace over long distances. Reading the break of the putt is less important for longer putts. If you can stroke the ball the right distance, the return putt will never be too testing, even if it has just missed to the side. Take a look at the broad break of the green and see what the putt will do in the last rotations of its roll – other than that, concentrate more on pace.

The long putt

1
The fundamentals do not change for any putt that you face. Adopt a good posture and keep the ball in the same position at address and swing the club at exactly the same pace for a short putt as you would a long one. Do not get tempted into hitting the ball harder – you need to maintain that smooth rhythm and tempo.

2
The only thing you should change in your putting stroke is the length of the backswing. If you have a longer putt, take the club back further. This will add momentum to the club-head, while maintaining control. Keep that tempo even for all putts, but by lengthening your backswing you will stroke the ball further.

3
Through impact and to a finish, maintain that natural tempo and rhythm. Your finish will be longer than for a shorter putt because you have lengthened your backswing. You must not have any body movement in the stroke. Simply rock your shoulders back and through while keeping your head still.

Practice drill

Aim for the killer zone

When you are faced with a long putt, you must keep your goals realistic – you are not going to hole-out regularly from 12m (40ft). Instead, aim to stop the ball in a 6m (20ft) killer zone beyond the hole. This will leave you with a tiny putt back and also gives the ball a chance of dropping. If you are short, you could never have holed the putt. As long as the ball is passing the hole, you might just get lucky.

1
Use your practice swings to better judge the pace of greens and cut out those frustrating three-putts. Once you have read the putt, concentrating on the 3m (10ft) nearest the hole, stand behind the ball, look at the hole and your ball and make practice strokes trying to find the right length of backswing for the putt.

2
Now move up to the ball. Practise next to it but keep your eye on the hole as you do, again trying to find the right length of backswing for the stroke. When it feels right, stand over the ball and use the stroke you just rehearsed. By looking at the hole as you prepare, your mind automatically judges the pace of the putt.

Short putts

You should never miss the shot from 2m (6ft) and closer. It is simple; just stand up to the ball and knock it into the hole. But all sorts of doubts can creep in, along with fear of failure and nerves. So developing a technique and thought process for short putts will help you cope with bouts of nerves and loss of confidence.

Confidence is the key

This simple exercise will instill confidence in your short-putt technique. On the practice green, drop some balls half-a-putter's length from the hole, which should be an unmissable distance. Knock these balls in. Get used to the idea of the ball actually dropping into the hole when you take the shot. Then move the ball back a few centimetres and knock those into the hole. If you miss at this stage, keep practising. Finally, finish with some 1-metre (3-foot) putts and keep practising these until they become second nature. You will feel more confident when you actually have to take a short putt in a real game.

Practise taking lots of shots from very close in and gradually move your practice balls further out until you are confident of making the short putt.

The short putt

1

From this short distance, you are looking to hole the putt; you should not be thinking about anything else, so this is an aggressive shot. For that reason, aim at the back of the hole. Take dead aim; you want to have a firm stroke as this will take the break out of the putt.

2

Keep the tempo of the putt the same as you take the club back and concentrate on the straight-back, straight-through, pendulum motion of the putterhead. This distance will expose an offline swing ruthlessly. You want to keep your lower body very still and accelerate the club-head towards impact.

3

Think of your follow-through for short putts. Imagine you are driving the putterhead down the line of the putt towards the hole. Finish with the putter aimed straight at the hole and keep your head completely still throughout. If you look up too early, you are in danger of moving your body and mishitting the stroke. Listen to the ball dropping; don't see it go in the hole.

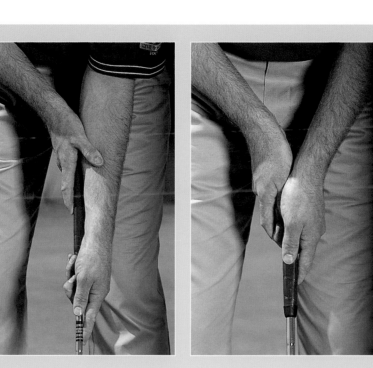

The dreaded yips

There is an affliction in golf called the yips that terrifies all players. Someone with the yips has an almost paralytic aversion to short putts. They cannot hole them. This leads to a freezing over the ball, where they are unable to take the club back, followed by an involuntary flinch which sends it yards past the hole. The yips can strike the best golfers; Bernhard Langer has overcome them three times and it is a pathological problem with on-going research looking into its causes and cures.

Langer defeated the yips by changing grips and practising hard. A change of technique does seem to offer a temporary solution – so if you suffer from this soul-destroying problem or if you ever develop it, get on the practice green and try out some new grips.

Dos and Don'ts

Do
✔ Aim at the back of the hole
✔ Stroke firmly to overcome break
✔ Concentrate on your follow-through
✔ Accelerate towards impact
✔ Listen to the ball drop

Don't
✘ Dribble it in the front of the hole
✘ Aim outside the hole
✘ Look to see the result of the putt
✘ Move your lower body during the stroke.

Putting routine

Golf is all about pressure. Once you have developed good fundamentals, coping when the heat is on determines whether you win or lose. Putting is the most pressurized part of this pressure-filled game, so you need all the tools and tricks possible to help you cope. A consistent pre-shot routine will make you confident of your technique, especially when the game is tight. It is important to have a pre-shot routine for every shot you play, but crucial when you are at the business end of the hole.

The universal routine

People have different routines – you must play with what makes you comfortable. There are a few ground rules (outlined opposite) that should be incorporated into any routine whether it is on the green or tee, but essentially you should do what feels best for you. When you are starting to play golf, don't take too long lining up your putts – there is nothing more annoying on the golf course than a slow player. You must have a routine, but keep it short yet unhurried.

The classic routine

1
First you must read the putt. Take your first look as you arrive on the green, gauging a general idea for the putt, then look at the putt from at least two angles, usually from behind the hole and behind the ball. You should have a good idea of the break by the time you are finished.

2
Take some practice swings from behind the ball, keeping an eye on the hole as you do. Try to picture in your mind the ball travelling up the break you have chosen and into the hole. When you have a clear image in your mind's eye, then you can stand up to the ball.

3

Take some final practice strokes, ensuring you have the swing right for the putt, place the putterhead behind the ball and take one last look at the hole. Stick with your preparation and observations, look back to the ball and within two seconds – no longer – pull the trigger.

4

Timing of a routine is crucial. You must take the same amount of time for every shot, whether it is your first putt of the round or a putt to win the Open. Your pre-shot routine must not change simply because of the match situation or you will undermine its whole purpose.

Copy big Jack

Jack Nicklaus, the winner of 18 major championships, was the king of pre-shot routines. You could set your watch by his routine; it would take exactly the same time for each shot, irrespective of the match situation. He would never hit a shot on the practice range without going through his routine. An important part was the visualization of the shot. Once, when he was about to play, a member of the crowd disturbed him so he stood away from the ball. He turned to the crowd and said: 'What a pity, that was a great shot I had lined up there.' The image of his ball soaring high and landing near the flag was so clear in his mind that there was never doubt about its outcome.

Practice drill
Make it routine

This may not sound like the most invigorating of exercises, but any time you are on the putting green or driving range, use a pre-shot routine for each shot you hit. Instead of aimlessly knocking balls at a hole 3m (10ft) away, take your time over each one, preparing as though it is a putt in anger. Good golfers all have a solid pre-shot routine that is so ingrained that it feels strange to play a shot without it.

Reading putts

Being able to read putts accurately is a skill that is learned the more golf you play. There are a few rules and hints that can help when trying to make an accurate read. Remember, the harder you hit the putt, the less the borrow (another word for break) will affect the ball. Similarly, the softer the putt, the more it will turn.

The harder you hit your putt, the less the borrow will affect the ball, allowing it to run straight.

Always play putts straight

It is one thing reading borrow confidently, but if you can't stroke the ball where you want then you will struggle to become a decent putter. In order to play break consistently, treat every putt as straight. That doesn't mean that you should aim right at the hole for each putt, but pick a point where the ball will turn on the green, a patch of worn grass or an old pitch-mark, and aim directly at this point. This will help you to avoid setting up inaccurately and mishitting.

The clues

1

There are clues all around the green to the break of that particular green. Use these clues to save you headaches and puzzlement when the ball starts to turn in the opposite direction to that which you expected. Take a look at the green and the lie of the land as you approach. Often the break is easier to spot from a distance than when you are on the putting surface.

2

Is the green carved out of a slope? If so, the ball is likely to break down the slope. This may sound obvious, but often when greens lie like this, they look flatter than they actually are. So keep an eye on slopes and make use of the clue the course is giving you.

Dos and Don'ts

Do

✔ Read the green as you approach

✔ Look at the putt from two angles

✔ Pay attention to slopes around greens

✔ Look for natural landmarks for clues

✔ Make each putt a straight putt

Don't

✘ Miss the low side of the hole

✘ Spend hours reading each putt

✘ Ignore the lie of the land.

3

Natural landmarks can often give you an idea about the lie of the land or break. Balls tend to turn towards water and away from mountains – so if you are putting on a lakeside green, take a line away from the water.

4

A common mistake that amateur golfers make is never giving a putt enough room to break. If you are going to miss a putt, try to miss it on the high side of the hole, as this means the ball is always turning towards the hole and has a chance of dropping, rather than slipping away from the cup. Miss the pro-side not the low-side.

Top tip

The late Payne Stewart used to overcome trouble with reading greens by picturing himself pouring a jug of water over the green. He would then watch in his mind's eye to see which way the water flowed in towards the hole. This gave him a clearer picture of the natural lie of the land and resulted in a more accurate read.

Practise putting

Practising putting can be a tedious task, but it is something all golfers need to do more often. The putter is the club you use most often in a round, yet it is the club we practise least. As part of the weekend's exercises, getting on to the putting green for an hour's practice is crucial. To make it more interesting, here are some practice drills and games that should brighten up the session.

Compass putting

Place four balls at the compass points around a hole, about 1m (3ft) out. Walk around each ball and sink the putt. Once you have holed all four in succession, move the balls further away. Keep moving them further back whenever you hole four in succession. This will give you a great variety of putts both in distance and break, as well as cranking up the pressure when you've been stuck at 2m (6ft) for 20 minutes.

Putt one-handed

This is a great tool for working on the smoothness of your stroke. Place a tee-peg on the putting surface, drop three balls about 2m (6ft) away and putt to the tee with only your right hand on the grip and your left behind your back. This will help your putterhead control and make you accelerate through the ball.

Putt ball beyond ball

Try this drill to help your distance judgement; it will also take the pressure off your short putts by improving your long putts:

1 Take around 12 balls and putt the first 5.5m (6yd) across the green.
2 Try to putt the next ball a metre beyond this. Then putt a third ball a metre beyond that point.
3 Keep putting all the balls the same distance beyond the previous.
4 Once you become good at stopping the ball at this distance beyond the previous ball, repeat the drill shortening the distance between each ball.

Place marker under ball

Many mishit putts are caused by golfers looking too early to see the result and moving their body in the stroke. If you keep your head still and looking at the same spot after you have struck, you will improve your consistency. To help with this, place a marker underneath your ball and focus on this as you putt. Keep your eyes on this marker after the ball has left the club-face.

Putt to a towel

If you are struggling to find good feel over longer putts, try this drill to build confidence:

1 Place three bag towels around the green in different spots.
2 Take around 10 balls and putt to one of the towels.
3 Putt the next ball to a different towel.
4 Putt until you have hit all 10 balls to alternate towels.

Putting to towels, as opposed to holes, helps you become less hole-obsessed. The target is bigger, so you develop confidence from increased accuracy. The variety ensures you don't become used to just one length of putt alone.

Putt between clubs

To develop a good straight back and straight-through repetitive stroke, give yourself a 2-metre (6-foot) putt, place two clubs parallel on the ground and parallel to the line of the putt, just more than a putterhead apart. Make as many as 50 putts, making sure you don't knock the clubs with your putter, grooving that accurate stroke.

Putting checklist

Grip
● Keep palms opposite each other
● Club through palm of hand
● Hands work as a unit

Posture and set-up
● Good athletic posture
● Knees flexed
● Ball slightly forward in stance
● Feet just under shoulder-width apart
● Align parallel to ball-to-target line

Stroke
● Straight back and straight-through stroke
● Keep your head still throughout
● Keep your lower body still
● Accelerate club to the target.

End of Day 2: Key reminders

Day 2 has concentrated on the shots of finesse, the imaginative strokes and, predominantly, the short game. The importance of the work you have done on Day 2 cannot be over-emphasized. Putting is the most neglected yet most crucial element to a round of golf. Chipping and pitching well will save you five shots and if you have the right techniques and attitudes to escaping trouble, you will be well on your way to good scores.

Here are key reminders for each of the four lessons you have been through in the second section of this book. Use it as a reference tool if and when your technique goes awry as well as a careful reminder for what you've just learned.

Lesson 5: Pitching and chipping

- Use orthodox grip for pitching, but choke down. Hold the club loosely
- Align just left of target to give room for swing
- Swing with arms and shoulders, rotating your upper body so back faces the target
- Have at least three wedges in bag to provide options for pitching
- Use orthodox grip for chipping as for full swing or putting grip as in chip-putt technique
- Place ball back in your stance with hands forward at address
- Align a touch left of target
- Swing by accelerating through ball keeping wrists firm and ahead of club
- Experiment with a variety of clubs.

Accelerating powerfully through the ball will lead to crisp consistent chips and pitches.

Lesson 6: Bunkers

Greenside

- Open club-face then form grip
- Align well left of target, but as club-face is open, this should point straight at pin
- Swing along line of body, not towards target
- Use sand-wedge or a lob-wedge

Fairway

- Use enough club to escape the lip
- For set-up do not shuffle feet in sand; have feet slightly closer together
- Choke down and hold the club tighter
- During swing have quiet lower body.

Playing from bunkers is all about damage limitation – think escape first, get close second.

Lesson 7: Trouble shots

- Set-up changes for most tricky lies; play ball off your right foot with your handsforward
- Choke down the grip and look to hit hard out of trouble
- In the swing, hinge your wrists quickly so you can dig to the bottom of ball. Swing hard to hit through any extra turf or foliage
- Be realistic about your goals and use the 7/10 rule when deciding to play a shot.

Lesson 8: Putting

- Find a comfortable grip – reverse overlap is the most popular
- Make sure putter is right length, that you like it and that you are not wowed by a price-tag or manufacturer
- Adopt good, comfortable posture at set-up with everything aligned at the hole
- Rock your shoulders in stroke while keeping arms, hands and body completely still
- Develop a pre-shot routine to help cope with pressure and improve feel
- Always practise putting – you can never practise it enough.

Don't be disheartened!

Golf is a game that becomes more complex the more you look into it. This is why it is such an enduring game. It is impossible to conquer golf, but once you've played enough, you'll have those moments where you feel you've won and that's what keeps us coming back. So don't be disheartened by bad shots and poor score; find time for practice and always remember that you are meant to be having fun.

Don't get greedy when you are playing a recovery shot, look to make bogey your worst score.

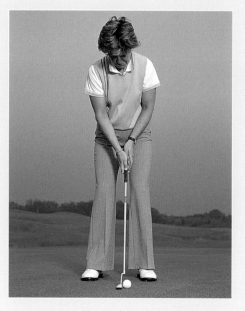

Putting is the most important part of the game. Build solid fundamentals and it becomes much easier.

Going forward

Now that you have an idea of how to hold the club, how to swing, how to putt, pitch and chip, how to play out of bunkers and trouble, you are probably feeling overloaded with information. It is hard to pick up all the elements of golf in a weekend – they take time to master.

In golf, experience and practice are everything, and learning through experience, both good and bad, is what makes this an addictive and engrossing sport. And then there is the trouble-shooting – no one is going to pick up a club and drill the ball straight down the course every time for ever. The rest of this book deals with everything from fault-fixing to game psychology.

Course management

This subject is all about how you carry yourself on the golf course, not only your physical well-being and preparation, but also your shot selection and thought processes for each element of the game. Sensible course management will make you more comfortable and confident during the round as well as saving you shots.

Course management is not only about physical well-being but also good shot selection.

Jargon busting

Slice When the ball curls right and out of control.
Hook When the ball curves out of control left after impact.
Push A shot that flies straight right, not curling.
Pull A shot that flies straight left, not curving in the air.
Fade A controlled shot that moves from left to right in the air.
Draw A controlled shot that moves from right to left in its flight.
Punch shot An intentionally played low-shot.

Fault fixing

Every golfer will suffer from what feels like an incurable fault at some point in their golfing lives. It may be a vicious slice, an angry hook or a disastrous shank. There are some common causes for these common afflictions, so the trouble-shooting section of this book will provide answers.

Advanced shots

The more golf you play, the more consistent your swing, the more you will want to develop other shots. Being able to work the ball around obstacles or into hidden parts of the green by shaping it from left to right or right to left in the air is a sophisticated skill. There are also a number of short-game shots that could just add that extra dimension to your game, helping you to pick up shots where you might have dropped them previously.

Practising well

It is great news if you have been down to the range hitting balls twice a week, but if you are not practising well, you will be doing your game more damage than good. Working on specific drills and thoughts as well as charting your success is all part of effective practice, so try these guidelines and add a purpose to your endeavours.

Practise specific techniques, rather than hitting aimless balls down the fairway. Specific drills will help hone your game.

Shot selection

Jack Nicklaus is the greatest golfer ever to have lived. He won more major tournaments than anyone in history and, barring even more remarkable achievements from Tiger Woods, he looks like remaining the all-time best. One of his great strengths was his course management and shot selection. It is often said that although he hit bad shots, he rarely hit the wrong shot – if you can be more like Jack in your course management and decision-making, even if you can't strike the ball half as well as him, you'll score well.

Preparation

Preparing well is crucial to hitting the course running. Turning up three minutes before your tee time, stumbling over your tee-shot and taking a seven on the first hole does not set you up for a fun day's golf. Here are some tips on how to prepare and warm up effectively.

Equipment preparation

Sort out your equipment the night before your round. Make sure you have enough balls, tees and gloves. Pack rain gear if it is going to be wet and count your clubs. It is especially easy to lose your putter, which you may have been practising with indoors – so make a careful note to check for the short stick. Other items you will need are:

- A hat or cap
- Provisions – a chocolate bar, banana and water
- Pitch-mark repairer and pencil
- Sun-cream or an extra sweater depending on the weather forecast.

Check your equipment before you set off. Your favourite golf balls should be clean and marked and your glove should show no signs of deterioration.

A planned warm-up will save you shots on the opening holes.

The perfect warm-up

Try to leave yourself at least 30 minutes to warm up before you tee off. Use this time to get your golfing muscles moving and switch your mind to the task at hand – remember that this is a warm-up not a practice and is no place to be working on technique. Here is an ideal routine:

- Spend 15 minutes on the range hitting a few balls with every club, starting with a wedge and working down to a driver, then back again. Work predominantly on hitting with a good rhythm.
- Go to the practice bunker and splash a few out of the sand. Don't worry about how close you leave them, just concentrate on escaping for five minutes.
- Spend five minutes hitting some short chips, just to warm up your short-game technique.
- Lastly, practise putting by holing a series of short putts. Hit a dozen 1-metre (3-foot) putts so that your body gets a good feel for the technique of actually sinking putts.

Ensure you have plenty of time for short-game practice before your round. This will give you a feel for the speed of the greens.

Pre-shot routine

1

A pre-shot routine is key to coping with any pressure. It provides familiarity and a mental bubble that you can retreat in to when the heat is on. First, stand behind the ball and visualize the shot you are attempting. Picture in your mind the ball flying exactly where you want it to, then dropping and finishing in the perfect spot.

2

Make some practice swings, using the exact swing that you intend to use for real. Keep that mental image of your ball soaring to the perfect spot as you practise. Do not take too many swings; just enough to make you feel loose and comfortable.

3

Set up to the ball by placing your club-head behind it first, ensuring that it is square to the intended target line. Now build your address, making sure you align everything correctly, make a few waggles of the club to keep loose, then take one final look at the target before looking back to the ball and pulling the trigger.

Dealing with first tee nerves

1 Breathe deeply as you make practice swings – breathe in on your backswing and out on your follow-through. Take as many as you need to feel the oxygen flowing around your body.
2 Hold the grip more loosely. When you are nervous, you automatically tense up. By loosening your grip, you will regain rhythm and tempo.
3 Add a waggle before hitting the ball. Keep moving the club-head before making a swing, to keep your muscles loose and relaxed.

Strategy

Most golf professionals will tell you that they could save any mid-handicap golfer at least five shots a round if they were able to caddy for them. Through simple, strategic shot selection, they could make a five-shot difference – so here are some of the common mistakes that golfers make on par-3s, par-4s and par-5s.

Stick to your strategy

Before a round, think your way through the course. What club will you take off which tee? From where do you want to hit each approach? Your preparation will offer you the best chance of scoring well on that hole; any change will damage your chances.

Jargon busting

Birdie A score on a hole that is one-under the par.
Eagle A score on a hole that is two-under the par.
Albatross A score on a hole that is three-under the par.
Bogey A score on a hole that is one-over the par.
Double bogey A score on a hole that is two over the par.
Laying up When you do not go for the green with your second or third shots, but intentionally play to a distance short of the green.

Par-3s
Short-siding yourself On any par-3, there is a good area to miss the hole and a bad. If you cannot go straight at the flag, pick the line that will leave you the easiest chip or putt, giving you the better chance of getting close, even if this shot is longer than the alternative.

Use the whole tee-box A par-3 gives you the luxury of having a perfect lie and options on line for an approach shot, so make use of this. If there are too many divots between tee markers, move two club-lengths back behind them to the smoother grass. Tee the ball up on the side that gives you the best line to the flag.

Par-4s

Always taking a driver Many golfers arrive on a par-4 and immediately reach for the long stick. This is foolish, especially on a short par-4 where the hole gets tighter closer to the green. Use a lofted wood or iron to take the trouble out of play and leave a full shot to it. Often it is easier to hit close with a full 9-iron than with a half-hit sand-wedge.

Par-5s

Many golfers think par-5: eagle Get there in two and sink the putt. This is a high-risk strategy as you will more often than not need a driver from the tee and a risky long-iron or fairway-wood for your second. Is the risk really worth the reward or would you be better laying up and perhaps pitching close for a one-putt birdie, two-putt par?

Not thinking about your second shot You must be as careful with your lay-up on a par-5 as you are with your tee-shot or approach. This shot will position your approach so don't get too greedy; pick a specific spot where you want to hit in from and stick to it.

Playing a new course

When playing a new course, you may feel lost and unsure of distances or hole layouts. Here are a few quick tips:

● Buy a course planner and have a word with the pros about tricky holes, the pace of the greens and characteristics of the course.

● Pay attention to yardage markers (often sprinkler heads), and trust them, even if your eye tells you otherwise.

● Check to see if yardages are marked to the front or middle of greens – there can be as much as three clubs' difference between front and back.

Psychology

The mind plays a huge role in making you a good golfer. The difference between the very good and very best golfers is generally recognized to be the power of the mind. Tiger Woods is mentally the strongest player on the planet, which goes alongside his immense athletic ability. Here are a few simple pieces of advice that could make all the difference to your score.

Play mini courses

A great way to cope with the highs and lows of any particular round is to split the 18 holes into six groups of the three mini courses. Work out what your score should be for each set of three holes. Then, if you have a bad run, you can restart and focus afresh on the next three holes and not worry about what has gone before. If you are two-over par for each group, then you are playing to a handicap of 12 – that makes it sound easy.

During a round, say things to yourself like: 'I am going to split the fairway here', or 'this is going to drop'. Mental attitude counts for a great deal in golf at all levels.

Let it out like Tiger

Anyone who doesn't get angry on the golf course is lying. We all lose our temper after a missed short putt or a duffed tee-shot and often it is good to let this anger out. Watch Tiger Woods after he's played a poor shot: he pulls his cap down over his mouth and swears to release frustration. As long as he's not too loud, this is a clever way to behave. So don't keep that anger in and stew miserably the whole round; discreetly let off steam and return to the job in hand.

Keeping cool on the course

Keep a level head
Try to keep calm through the bad moments of a round and, crucially, through the good times. Staying level in your mind is the key to consistent golf. Accept the bad shots and, similarly, don't get too carried away if you chip in. If your heart is pumping with excitement or anger, it is hard to play a sensible following shot.

Enjoy the space between shots
A shot takes around two minutes to play. That means you will have a lot of time in between shots to switch off and relax and it is important to do so. No one can concentrate solidly for four hours, so make a point of taking your mind away from the game and either chat to your partner or juggle balls while you wait. This will help you focus on the next shot and forget the one gone, however good or bad.

Walk like a winner
If you walk tall and proud with your chest out and head held high, you are able to trick your mind into thinking the way you look is actually the way you are.

Psychology checklist

Preparation
● Sort out equipment the night before
● Spend 30 minutes warming up before tee time
● Warm-up is a warm-up, not a practice.

Strategy
● Stick to your pre-match game plan
● Use the whole tee-box on par-3s
● Use a variety of clubs from par-4 tees
● Make use of strokes on tough par-4s
● Don't always go for par-5s in two.

Psychology
● Break the round into six mini courses
● Stay level-headed throughout
● Relax between shots
● Walk like a winner.

The slice

A slice is the most common problem for golfers – more people lose their ball with a vicious curling shot out right than anywhere else. Understanding exactly how a slice is caused will take you a long way towards righting the problem. Usually, it is down to faulty fundamentals.

Basic slice causes

Most slices are caused by technique problems at address. Here are some of the more common mistakes.

Club in the palm of your hand
When you take your grip, you want the club to run through the bottom of your fingers on your left hand. If the club lies more in the palm of your left hand, then you will find it hard to bring the club-face square to the ball at impact. You restrict your hand movement, causing the club-face to be open at impact and the result is a slice.

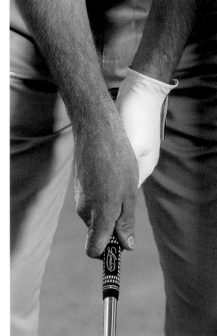

What is a slice?

If your club-head swings from outside the target line to cutting in across the ball, and the club-face is open (aiming right of the target), you will hit a slice. Imagine you are playing a sliced forehand tennis shot, you cut underneath the ball, imparting left-to-right sidespin. This is exactly what happens when you hit a slice in golf,

only you are using a golf ball and golf club. The result is the ball that starts left and curls immediately right and out of control.

Alignment wrong at address
When you have sliced a few, you will instinctively aim further left. And then you'll slice it even worse. This does not help: it actually accentuates your slice. If you aim left, then you will swing the club down the line of your body, which will be from out-to-in. As soon as you swing from out-to-in you will slice the ball. If you can bear it, aim straight and you'll hit straighter shots.

Weak grip
If your grip is too weak – if you can't see any knuckles on your left hand – then you may find it difficult to bring the club-head square to the ball at impact. Strengthen your grip so that you can see more knuckles, which will close the club-face at address, and you'll straighten that curve.

Slice cures

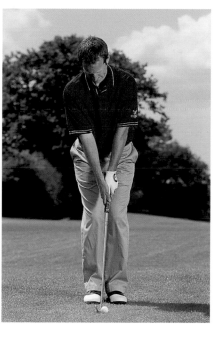

Work on set-up
Make sure your grip is neutral, that the ball is not too far forward in the stance, that you are aligned square to the target and the club-head is pointing directly where you want to hit. Working with a mirror and reference manuals can help you drill yourself into a comfortable, natural position.

Feet together drill
A driver is a slicer's worst enemy, so for this drill you must not use it. Take a 7-iron, tee a ball up low and stand to it with your feet close. Now try to hit the ball off the tee from this position using your normal swing. Slicers will find this hard, as they will over-balance. Practise until you can strike cleanly from this position then replicate that swing once you are over the ball.

Barrier drill
A slice swing is when the club is too far away from your right side on the downswing, which causes you to cut across the ball and slice. Put a headcover just behind the ball, then hit shots avoiding that headcover on your downswing. If you smash into the headcover, then you have swung on the wrong path – you want to miss it on the side on which you are standing – inside the line.

If you cannot straighten your drives, try this extreme on-course solution. Aim right of the target, just where you don't want your ball to go. When your body sees a closed club-face, it automatically adjusts – your unconscious swing tries to hit the ball right. By opening the club-face, your unconscious swing works in the opposite direction – attempting to hit left, giving you a better chance of a straight shot.

The hook

A hooked shot will always travel further and bury itself deeper into the rough than a slice but a hook is a less bad fault – it means you are using your hands through the ball, but it still needs to be straightened out. Most hooks are caused by problems at address. Here are some of the more common mistakes.

What is a hook?

A hooked ball starts down the middle of the fairway, then curves powerfully left, bouncing across three fairways or burying itself in a bush. It is caused by the club-head being closed at impact (aiming left) after the club has swung from inside the line to out.

Basic hook causes

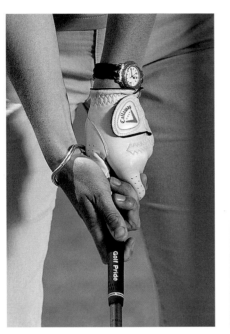

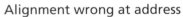

A strong grip
If you cannot see any knuckles on your right hand and four knuckles on your left, then you have a strong grip which could be causing your hook. You want to be able to see two knuckles on your left hand and the 'V' in your right should point to your right collar bone. This small adjustment will feel horrible to start with, but perseverance will make it feel more natural.

Alignment wrong at address
If you are hooking the ball, you may well find yourself aiming right of the target to allow for sharp curl left. This will make you swing too much from the inside which will cause a hook. Try to square everything to the target at address: your knees, shoulders and feet with the club-face aiming straight.

Weight
At address you want to have the ball forward in your stance – a hook could result because the ball is too far back – and keep your weight even across your feet. Leaving too much weight on your left side in your set-up can lead to a hooked shot.

Three hook cures

Club in front drill

Once you have sorted out your solid alignment and good fundamentals, work on your swing to stop hooking. Go down to the range with this one thought in your mind: 'Have the club-head in front of me throughout my swing.' Check each position in your swing – has the club-head gone behind your back at the top of your backswing, or is it above your head? Does the club go behind your legs in your initial movement?

Left foot back

Set up to the ball naturally, as square to the target as possible. Move your left leg back by a foot. This will give you a very open stance: you will be aiming well left of the target. Make normal swings from this position. The altered set-up will make it difficult to swing from inside as you will swing along your body line, which is more likely to cause a slice than a hook. Reset yourself after a bucket of balls and replicate that feeling.

Umbrella drill

Place a barrier, such as an umbrella stuck in the ground, a metre behind the club-head at address. Take some practice swings, taking the club back but avoiding the barrier. A player who hooks will be taking the club away on the inside, which would hit the umbrella. This practice forces you to keep the club-head either outside the line, or away from the body, on the takeaway.

A push and hook are similar

A push – a ball hit straight right (see page 108) – and a hook may seem completely different to each other, but they are often caused by the same faults in the swing. Similarly, a slice and a pull often originate from similar problems.

Pushes and hooks result from an in-to-out swing path – the club travels from inside the target line to outside. If your club-face is square to the swing path when you make contact, you will push or block the ball right. If the club-face is aiming left, you will be putting topspin on the ball and hooking it left.

The push and pull

Pushes and pulls are not as devastating as hooks and slices but can be equally frustrating, especially as you often hit the ball well only to see it disappear right or left.

Basic causes
Pushes and pulls are, by and large, caused by the same problems as hooks and slices (see pages 104–7). The following are a few common set-up faults that make you push and pull.

What is a push?

A push is a shot that flies straight right of the target as opposed to curving, like a sliced shot. It is caused by a swing that approaches impact from too close to the golfer and the club-face is square to this line of attack.

What is a pull?

A pull is the opposite – it flies straight left without curling. The club comes towards impact away from your body, like a slice, with the face square to this swing path, pulling the ball right.

Aligning your body correctly will avoid most pushes and pulls.

Causes of pushes and pulls

Push
Everything might be well lined up, but your shoulders have drifted right, shutting your body to the target a touch. This mis-alignment may be accentuated when you make a full swing pushing the ball right. The longer the club, the further right it is liable to fly.

Pull
You could be pulling the ball because of alignment problems. You may have set your feet, knees and hips square to the ball-to-target line but if your shoulders are aligned left, you could be in danger of pulling the ball left. So set up to the ball, place a club across your shoulders and make sure that it is parallel to the target line.

Push cure set-up

Pull cure set-up

A push or a pull can often seem less severe than a hook or slice (although not in every case); the cause can be simple and easy to fix. You may just be closing (aiming left) or opening (aiming right) the club-face at address. So as a final check, make sure your club-face points straight down the target line. It may only be a few millimetres or inches at address, but when the ball reaches its target, it could be much more.

1
Place the club to the ball with your right hand alone, which will help you align your shoulders further left than before. Now build the rest of your set-up by placing your feet, knees and hips in position.

2
Place your left hand on the club. Don't worry if this feels odd; if you are used to aiming right, the change may well feel awkward. Keep the ball forward in your stance – if it creeps back, you may end up pushing the ball.

If you suffer a succession of pulls, try the mirror image of the set-up for a push. Put the club behind the ball with only your left hand on the grip. Don't let the ball position slide too far forward, align yourself to the target line and drop your right hand on the club, which will bring your shoulders into a square position.

Problem chips

Everyone knows the horror of a fluffed chip, watching the ball trickle a few metres in front of you, leaving you – ignominiously – with almost the same shot. Chipping can be the most rewarding and distracting element of the game, so ironing out the fluffs and mistakes can make a massive difference to your score.

Slipping up with a chip

Well we all know what it is, the ball barely moves and you are faced with more dropped shots, but what exactly happens? The club, instead of making contact with the ball, takes turf first – the base of the swing occurs too early – so all the energy in the club-head drives into the ground and not the ball.

Two basic causes

1

A common problem can be ball position. If the ball is too far forward in your chipping stance, opposite your left foot for instance, then you will find it difficult to hit the ball with a descending blow. You want to hit down on the back of the ball crisply, catching ball first then turf. This proves difficult if you are having to reach for it because of a faulty ball position at address.

2

Golfers not trusting the loft of the club can often cause a duff or 'heavy contact' chip. The design of the golf club is there to help the golfer. All the player must do is make a smooth stroke with the correct technique and let the loft do the work. If the golfer tries to help the shot by scooping with the wrists then he or she is in danger of either catching too much turf or hitting the ball half way up and thinning it through the back of the green. Keep your wrists solid to avoid this.

Chip cures

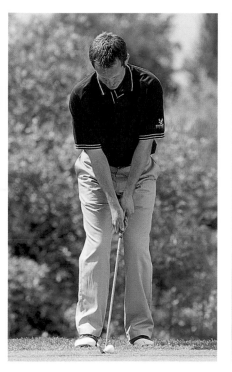

Keep hands ahead of the ball
Once you have developed a decent set-up position (see page 62), you will have placed the ball back in your stance, with your feet together and your hands ahead of the ball. Try to return to this position at impact. Take the club back, retaining that angle between your wrists and the club shaft, then swing through, recreating your address position at impact.

Follow-through
If you decelerate the club-head towards impact, you will suffer a heavy contact chip. Slowing down or hesitating in your swing is a common problem and the cause of most fluffed chips. To avoid this, concentrate on your follow-through. Imagine you want your hands to swing 20 per cent further through than back.

Finish
If you swing so that your hands do not get higher than your hips but are a few centimetres below, hold a finish position just above your waist, keeping your hands ahead for as long as possible. You would use this swing for a longer chip, but it will help concentrate your mind into accelerating through impact and avoiding a poor chip.

Advanced shots

Once you have mastered the basic swing, to take your game to the next level you need to be more creative and versatile with the shots you hit. This section looks at more complex shots, how to play them and why they are useful. First up, shot-shaping.

The fade

A fade is a shot that starts to the left of the fairway and curls right in the air. The big difference between a fade and a slice is that a fade is intentional and under control! This is a handy shot to have for a number of situations. If you are trying to hit close to a flag that is tucked behind a bunker to the right of the green, you can work the ball in from the left. If you have hit slightly offline or are facing a dog-leg (a hole with a sharp turn), you can slide the ball around any obstacles and get close.

Being able to play a fade can help you get closer to tight pins and recover after wayward shots.

Achieving a fade

 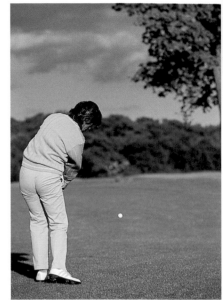

Address changes

This may sound like a difficult stroke to execute, and it does require practice, but essentially the only difference between this swing and your normal swing is at address. Put the ball further forward in your stance, align your body left of the target – along the line you want to start the shot – and square your club-face to the target. Your body aligns where you want the ball to begin its flight, your club-face aims where you want the ball to finish.

The swing

Once you have made these alterations to your set-up, you must swing normally. All the initial adjustments will make you swing along the line of your body, with a slightly out-to-in swing path. This will cause the fade automatically so there is no need to adjust your swing. In fact, if you do try to help the ball from left-to-right, you could end up shanking or pulling badly.

The draw

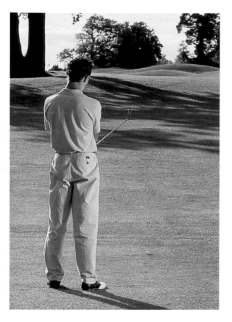

What is it and when to play it?
The draw is a controlled shot that moves from right to left in the air. It will fly and run further than a fade and has less backspin. If you want to hit a long drive, a booming draw is the perfect shot, especially if it follows the shape of the fairway. As well as helping you work the ball around obstacles or into tight pins, a draw is a handy shot to be able to play into the wind as it drills through the air.

Address changes
The address change is the opposite to those needed to produce a fade. Align your feet and shoulders right of the target line, aim the club-face square. If you want to draw the ball more, aim further right, but always keep that club-face pointing at the target. Remember, similarly to the fade, aim the club where you want the ball to finish and align your body where you want it to start.

The swing
The swing will again be dictated by these set-up changes, so you will naturally swing from in to out and put draw-spin on the ball.

Release
For this shot, it is crucial not to hesitate. You must swing aggressively through and make a good, full release with your hands (see page 52); that is, turn your right hand over your left through impact.

Hitting high and low shots

To score well in all conditions, and especially when it is windy, you must have versatility beyond the reach of your clubs alone. Knowing how to alter your swing to manipulate your ball flight is an important tool in conquering all types of golf courses and adds a new and exciting dimension to the game.

The best players in the world use ball flight to hit it closer to flags, and the more you improve, the more you will learn the importance of controlling ball flight.

Hitting high shots

The set-up
If you are playing downwind and want to make the most of it, or are trying to play over a tall tree, you may find yourself trying to hit the ball high. The first thing to do is push the ball forward in your stance, then stand closer and more upright. This will encourage a steeper swing and will have the effect of adding loft to the club without losing any distance to the ball.

The swing
Make a natural and normal swing. The ball will fly higher than before, but stay behind it at impact longer than normal. Don't scoop the ball in the air with your hands as this will lead to either a duff, a thin or simply a weak shot that finishes short.

Swing aggressively at the ball. The more club-head speed you generate, the more spin you put on the ball and the higher it flies. Hesitation will lead to a mishit.

The finish
Signify your aim for the shot in your finish position by making a full finish with your hands held high above your head. A good thought for this shot is to try and reach that high-finish position for a proper strike.

The punch shot

The set-up
You may want to hit a low-punch shot if you are hitting into the wind or if you want to run the ball up the green to a pin that is cut at the back. This is a great shot as it offers control under pressure and is low risk, once you've practised it. Place the ball back in your stance, with your feet slightly closer together and move your hands forward so the shaft points towards the target.

The swing
With your weight at address evenly spread, the set-up alterations will make the swing steeper. Try to drill the ball low to the ground with a more compact and shorter swing. Use less lower body, but turn your back to the target and then forward through impact. Although you are trying to drill the ball low into the air, hold the club lightly and swing positively.

The finish
Hold a truncated finish that reflects your aim of pinning the ball low. The low-shot is one that Tiger Woods uses to great effect when he plays links golf and he holds that very distinct and short finish position. Add a bit of Tiger to your finish.

Choosing the right shot

Picking the right shot to play at the right time is one of golf's great skills and one that is learnt through (often harsh) experience. For any given shot there are a number of different ways of getting the ball close to the hole – it is a matter of selecting the best one for you. For example, Tour pros hit low shots into greens with the pins at the back and high pitches when they are at the front – they will play fades to keep away from trouble and high draws for extra distance. Seeing the shot and being able to visualize it before you play is half the battle and something not everyone can master – this is why Seve Ballesteros was such a genius.

Short-game shots

The basic chip shot is a fundamental technique for any golfer, but the more you play, the more you find situations where, good as the basic chip is, it is tricky to guarantee getting the ball dead. This may be thanks to a tangling lie, or a tough pin placement, so here are a few alternative short-game techniques that will help you out of tricky spots.

The lob shot

The set-up
If you need to chip over a bunker to a pin that is cut close to the edge, not giving you too much green to work with, you'll need to lob the ball high in the air and land it softly next to the hole – the lob shot. Take a lob-wedge, align left of the target (open your stance) and flex your knees. This is a tough shot if you are playing from a bare lie or a firm fairway – it is best to play it when the ball sits up slightly in fluffy rough.

The swing
Swing along the line of your feet and cut right underneath the ball with an open club-face, which will exaggerate the loft. The ball will fly high in the air and land softly (with no run or spin). This is a high-risk shot which means it is foolish to play from the wrong lie. You must be aggressive, otherwise you will thin the ball.

Bellied-wedge

The set-up
This is a clever shot that will initially make your partner think you've made a mess, but will finish close, making them think it was a fluke. When your ball is between two cuts of rough on the fringe of the green, it is hard to hit the ball with the full face of the wedge consistently. Instead, strike the ball halfway up with the leading edge of the club-head. Set it back in your stance and use your putting grip.

3-wood chip

Use your putter everywhere

Golfers do not make the most of their putters. There are situations all over golf courses where the putter is the best option, but it doesn't even cross some golfers' minds. If you don't have to clear any long grass or obstacles, why lift the ball in the air? A bad putt will always be closer than a bad chip, and a good putt is usually dead. So next time you are eyeing up an 18-metre (30-yard) chip-and-run, or even playing from a shallow-faced greenside bunker, think of your putter and try it out.

The swing
Now treat the shot like a putt, rolling it out of the tricky lie and smoothly on to the green. Strike the ball with the blade of your club, which will cut through the entangling rough easily and avoid heavy contact. Using your putting technique gives greater control and feel.

The set-up
When you are on the fringe around the green, playing a chip with a 3- or 5-wood is an option made popular by Tiger Woods. Using a fairway-wood stops the ball becoming stuck in an entanglement of damp grass. Choke down a 3-wood then adopt your normal chipping set-up. You need to be further away from the ball than usual.

The swing
Make a normal putting stroke with this set-up, rocking your shoulders back and through the ball. Use the length of your backswing to judge the length of the chip; swing further back for a longer shot. Try to use as little wrist and lower body as possible, keeping the club-head low to the ground throughout.

Practising perfection

Playing golf is easy – playing golf well requires practice; lots of practice. But it is not simply spending the hours on the range that turns you into Nick Faldo overnight. You need to practise effectively to make the most of your dedication – otherwise you'll be disappointed.

Three golden rules

Bad practice

Overusing the driver Golfers often turn up to the range, hit 100 balls with their driver and go home. This will not help your game – there are 13 other clubs to work with.

Quantity not quality Putting the hours in is good, but if your practice is aimless, you will be practising aimless shots. You need a purpose and focus – quality not quantity – so use the golden rules listed opposite.

Wrong practice Make sure you are practising a suitable technique. If you work hard with your faulty swing, your faulty swing will be difficult to mend – practice makes permanent not perfect.

1
Practise with a purpose
Each time you go down to the range, have a focus for your practice. It may be your driving, short-irons, rhythm, set-up or specific swing-change, but you must have at least one goal that you are working towards. Endless buckets of meaningless balls produces a meaningless swing, so practice with a purpose.

2
Make it routine
You can work on your routine whatever you are practising. Every time you set-up to hit a shot, run through your pre-shot routine as though you are on the course hitting a shot in anger. This will make you focus and think about the shot more clearly as well as ingraining that routine – you want it to become more difficult to hit a shot without it than with it.

3

Always have a target
A driving-range is not the prettiest element of a golf course – often it is a bleak field disappearing towards the horizon. When you are hitting balls, it does not matter what element of the game you are working on, pick a target. When do you hit a shot during a round that is not at a target? Never, so don't do it on the range; all you are doing is practising bad habits.

Focus your thoughts...

A great way to develop confidence and make the most of your practice time, especially before a competition, is to play the course in your mind. If you usually play the first hole with a driver then an 8-iron, picture the shots in your mind and play them in turn, first hitting your driver, then your 8-iron. If you would have missed the green, practise a pitch in and so on.

Complete a whole round like this and mark out an imaginary score depending on how well you struck the ball, where it finished, if you pitched close and adding an (honest) number of putts. You can complete a round in 20 minutes, so start again and try to beat your score. This dress rehearsal in your mind will serve as an excellent guide out on the course.

Practice threshold – we are all different

When it comes to practice, all golfers are different. Some love nothing more than to stand at the range and beat buckets of balls until their hands blister and their backs ache. Others couldn't think of anything worse. Everyone needs to practise but there is no point doing it for two hours if you are bored after 30 minutes – it won't help your game. Colin Montgomerie won seven European Tour Order of Merits with minimal practice. This was his way, yet Padraig Harrington reached the top 10 in the world with endless hours on the range. We all have a practice threshold and it is pointless to go beyond it.

Good practice

To help with your focus, outlined on these two pages are five drills that work on various aspects of the swing. Each works well at eliminating one of many common swing problems – add them to a practice routine to sharpen your technique.

As with any sport, practice is key to overcoming problems and making good techniques regular and repetitive. Drills add a focus to your sessions and break up what can be a monotonous and, at times, thankless task.

Umbrella on backswing

To help with good weight transfer on your backswing – a common problem for many golfers – stick an umbrella in to the ground behind you, angled towards your right hip. Try to touch it with that hip as you take the club back: if you don't manage it, then your weight is stuck on your left side and you could be in trouble. So work on touching the umbrella with your right side as you swing back. It is important to turn the upper half of your body as you swing back, otherwise you will struggle for power and could end up hitting sliced and weak shots.

Feet together

This drill appeared early in the book, but it is such a useful exercise for so many parts of the swing that it is worth revisiting. Simply hitting balls with your feet close together will help your balance and ball striking, as well as cutting out excessive use of your lower body. If you are finding it tough to start with, then only use a 7-iron and tee the ball up. Return to this drill if your striking is off-centre as it is so useful for fine-tuning and regaining feel.

One-handed drill

Practise hitting balls with your right hand only to improve timing and help with full release. The right arm is an important element in timing a golf ball well. Make practice swings with your right arm alone, brushing the grass until you are used to the feeling. Now hit shots – this is tough so don't worry about shanks and tops to start with. Your body will adjust and you'll start hitting the ball cleanly, which is great for your swing.

Gateway drill

If you are fighting a slice or seem to be mishitting too many drives, improve your striking with this brutal drill. If 12 o'clock is your target line and your ball is the centre of a clockface, place two balls either side of yours at 10 o'clock and 4 o'clock, as illustrated, creating a gateway for the club to swing through. Try to hit the object ball without touching the two others. This will encourage you to swing slightly from inside the line, as opposed to outside which causes a slice, and once you've got the hang of this drill your ball striking will improve.

Line of balls – rhythm drill

Place about five balls on tees in a line a few centimetres apart, heading away from you. Using a short-iron, stand to the first ball and hit it with a short swing. Don't worry about where it finishes; without stopping walk down and hit the next ball, and then the next until you have hit them all. You are trying to build natural rhythm as you walk down the line so never let your club-head stop. Look to strike all the balls within 15 seconds, working on tempo as you hit. This is a liberating practice that is great for rediscovering rhythm.

Short-game practice

As you will have gathered by now, your full-swing is only half the game. Once you are on and around the green, the game is about touch, feel and short-game technique. Yet this part of the game is often ignored in practice, so here are five drills to make your short-game practice fun and effective.

A solid short game will enhance your long game – if you are not scared of missing greens, you are more likely to hit them, so any short practice you do has a knock on effect with the rest of your game.

Short-game drills

  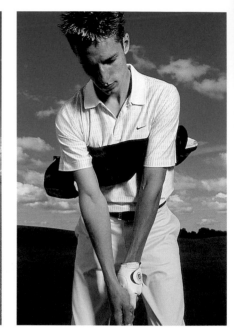

Match your swing length
To control the length of your chip shots and pitches, you want to keep your tempo even (don't try to hit the ball harder) but lengthen or shorten your backswing depending on the length of the chip. To help, place a line of balls running away from a practice green in a straight line a couple of metres apart.

Walk to the ball closest to the green and chip it close, using solid technique and even tempo. Now move back to the ball behind and hit this close, with a longer backswing but even swing speed. Keep moving back until you have chipped or pitched all the balls and you'll find your touch improving.

Towel under arms
To stop your pitching technique becoming too wristy, which could easily lead to inaccurate shots, place a towel under your arms and hit short pitches, keeping it in place through the shot. This drill will help keep the connection between your arms and body, so you don't let your hands and wrists overtake the shot. You are looking to turn your upper body, shoulders and arms back and through in sync.

Club-head cover behind ball

To help chip cleanly, you must hit down on the back of the ball. When you are practising, place a headcover 20cm (8in) behind the ball. Use a pitching-wedge and take your normal chipping stance. Now hit longish chips, around 9m (30ft), trying to avoid contact with the headcover. This will encourage you to hit down aggressively and will stop you using your wrists.

Throw balls for variety

Pitching and chipping practice is good, but in any given round you will find yourself in a variety of positions around the green. You will not always have that perfect lie or a clean line to the hole, so practising from endless perfect chipping positions is not ideal.

To create the variety of shots that you might find in a round, take a dozen balls and find a quiet green. Face the pin and lob all the balls over your shoulder so they land in different and varying positions beside the putting surface. Go to each ball and prepare as though it is a shot in anger and you are trying to leave yourself a short putt.

Chip to an umbrella

If you are having trouble with length and line on your pitches and chips, grab your umbrella out of the bag, open and upturn it. Now practise hitting chips into the umbrella to improve control of line and length. If you can land it in and around an umbrella-sized target on the green, you are going to finish close often.

Glossary

To save endless flicking through the book, here is a quick A–Z of golf, incorporating all the Jargon Busting featured.

A

Albatross a score on a hole that is three-under the par

Alignment where your body and club-head aim before you swing

B

Birdie a score on a hole that is one-under the par

Bladed irons old fashioned clubs with a straight back

Bogey a score on a hole that is one-over the par

Break or borrow the slopes on the green that will affect your ball's roll

Bunker a crater-like depression in the ground filled with sand designed to catch your ball. They may be placed around the green or on the edge of fairways

C

Cavity backed irons modern clubs with a hollow back

Chip-and-run chip shot that rolls most of the way to the hole

Chip-in holing a chip shot

Closed or shut club-face or body aims to the right of the target line

Club-head the part of the club that is used to strike the ball

Club-head speed how fast your club-head travels as you hit the ball

Coil as you turn your shoulders on the backswing, keep the lower half of your body as still as you can – the difference creates resistance known as coil

D

Divot a hole in the grass

Double bogey a score on a hole that is two-over par

Draw a controlled shot that moves from right to left in its flight

Driver the club that hits the ball the furthest

E

Eagle a score on a hole that is two-under the par

F

Fade a controlled shot that moves from left to right in the air

Fairway closely mown grass from where you hit your second or third shots

Fatting hitting too much turf before the ball

Fore! what you shout as a warning if your ball looks like hitting another golfer

Fringe slightly longer grass around the edge of the green

G

Gimme a term used in matchplay when a player concedes his opponent's short putt because it is so close he will not miss

Green the closely mown area with the hole cut on it. You use your putter on the green

Grip either the hold you have on the club or the rubber end of the club that you hold

H

Hazards bunkers, streams and lakes are hazards on the golf course

Honour, the whoever wins the previous hole has the honour and tees off first on the next hole

Hook when the ball curves out of control to the left after impact

I

Impact the moment the club-head hits the ball in the swing

Inside the line the side of the target line where you stand

Irons make up the bulk of your equipment and are numbered 3–9

L

Laying up when you do not go for the green with your second or third shots, but intentionally play to a distance short of the green

Lie how the ball sits on the grass

Lob where the ball flies most of the way to the hole

Loft the angle the club sits at relative to the perpendicular and which determines the ball's flight

M

Matchplay a format of the game where whoever wins the most holes, wins the match

N

Neutral grip grip that allows the hands to work in unison in the swing with neither having more influence than the other

O

Open club-face or body aims left of the target line

Out of bounds if you strike your ball over the boundaries of the course, you have hit the ball out of bounds

Outside the line the opposite side of the line to that on which you stand

Overswing when the club is swung too far in the backswing, causing a loss of power

P

Pin a flag marking where the hole is cut

Pitch-mark the mark your ball makes when it lands on the green

Posture how you stand to the ball; the shape your body takes at address

Provisional ball if you think you may lose the ball you have just played, you can play a second, or provisional ball

Pull a shot that flies straight left, not curving in the air

Punch shot an intentionally played low-shot

Push a shot that flies straight right, not curling

Putter the club you use on the green for rolling the ball into the hole

R

Reading the green to putt accurately you need to 'read' the break and borrow on the green

Release the rotation of your forearms and wrists after impact

Rescue club a hybrid wood and iron club without too much loft

Rough long grass that bounds the fairways and the greens

S

Semi-rough an area between the fairway and rough, where the grass is longer than the fairway but shorter than the rough

Shaft the part of the club that attaches the grip to the clubhead

Shallow swing this is when the club-head returns to the ball at impact level to the ground, hitting the ball on the upward part of the swing

Slice when the ball curls right and out of control

Square this can refer to the club-face or to your body. Your club-face is square if it is aimed directly at the target line. Your body is square when your shoulders, knees and toes are all aligned parallel to the ball-to-target line

Stance how wide your feet are and your ball position at address

Steep swing the opposite of a shallow swing where the club hits down on the back of the ball from an acute angle, relative to the ground

Strokeplay a format of the game where you compete to see who goes round the course in the lowest number of strokes

Strong grip a grip that makes the hands too prominent in the swing

T

Target line or ball-to-target line an imaginary line from where you want to hit to the ball

Tee-box flat areas with markers from where you hit your first shot on each hole

Topping hitting the top half of the ball

U

Up-and-down a chip, pitch or bunker escape followed by one putt to hole out. Usually, you have hit the ball dead and left yourself a small putt or gimme

W

Weak grip a grip that makes it hard to use hands through the swing

Wedges shorter clubs that come with various degrees of loft

Woods the biggest-headed clubs used for hitting distance

Y

Yips, the an affliction where golfers cannot hole short putts, leading to freezing over the ball, inability to take the club back or an involuntary flinch which sends the ball yards past

Index

Acknowledgments

Executive Editor Trevor Davies
Executive Art Editor Leigh Jones
Editor Charlotte Wilson
Designer Peter Gerrish
Production Controller Ian Paton
Photographer Angus Murray

Special photography
© Octopus Publishing Group/Angus Murray

Other photography
Getty Images/Scott Halleran 41 right

The Publisher would like to thank **East Sussex National** for permission to use the golf course for photography. We would also like to thank **Sarah MacLennan**, the Golf Pro at East Sussex National for taking part in the photo shoot, and also **Richard Higgins**, **Mark Jenkins**, **James Morrall**, **Debbie Morley**, **Holly Morley** and **Jessica Morley**